BITCOIN AND

BEGINNERS

TRADING BOTS, CANDLESTICK PATTERS
AND
TRADING PSYCHOLOGY

BORIS WEISER

Disclaimer

This book is produced with the goal of providing information that is as accurate and reliable as possible. Regardless, purchasing this book can be seen as consent to the fact that both the publisher and the author of this book are in no way experts on the topics discussed within and that any recommendations or suggestions that are made herein are for entertainment purposes only. Professionals should be consulted as needed before undertaking any of the action endorsed herein. Under no circumstances will any legal responsibility or blame be held against the publisher for any reparation, damages, or monetary loss due to the information herein, either directly or indirectly. This declaration is deemed fair and valid by both the American Bar Association and the Committee of Publishers Association and is legally binding throughout the United States. The information in the following pages is broadly considered to be a truthful and accurate account of facts and as such any inattention, use or misuse of the information in question by the reader will render any resulting actions solely under their purview. There are no scenarios in which the publisher or the original author of this work can be in any fashion deemed liable for any hardship or damages that may befall the reader or anyone else after undertaking information described herein. Additionally, the information in the following pages is intended only for informational purposes and should thus be thought of as universal. As befitting its nature, it is presented without assurance regarding its prolonged validity or interim quality. Trademarks that are mentioned are done without written consent and can in no way be considered an endorsement from the trademark holder.

Table of Contents

Introduction

This book focuses on bitcoin and cryptocurrencies trading and reveals various techniques and strategies. First, we are going to take a look at Margin Trading Features, Lending, Borrowing and Spot Trading Step-by-step on dYdX. After that, we will take a look at how Trading BOTs operate such as TradeSanta, Shrimpy, Gunbot, Crypto Hopper and 3commas. Next, we are going to look at Key metrics signals & Red flags, Volume, Liquidity and Artificial Perception of Demand. Next, you will learn about Trading tools such as Interest earning tool, a VISA Cash back Card on Crypto.com. Next, you will learn step by step how to do a 100x Altcoin Research. Here, you will learn about Screening Process, Trading Volume & Exchange activity. You will also learn how to identify Onchain Metrics, Development Activity, Project Uniqueness, Adoption & Community Support. Next, you will learn about Trading Tips such as Option Moneyness, Put Call Ratio, Options Skew, Market Parameters and Options Expiry Dates. Moving on, you will learn about Bullish Candlestick Patterns, Bearish Candlestick Patterns and Continuation Candlestick Patterns. After that, we will comprehend what is Implied Volatility, why Implied Volatility is Important and what is an Implied Volatility Rank. Next, you will learn about Trading Psychology such as Gambler's Fallacy, Confirmation Bias, The law of Small Numbers, The Survivorship Bias, Correlation, Hindsight Bias, Recency & Attribution Bias and Sung Cost Fallacy. After that, you will learn what separates Winning traders from Loosing Traders. Lastly, you will how to create a Step by step checklist for a Trading Plan and how to set up a Trade Order. If you are ready to jump on board, let's begin by looking at dYdX Margin Trading Features.

Cryptocurrencies are all about decentralization. Individual control of our assets that no one can restrict or seize. Yet it's always puzzled me why seemingly decentralized assets are overwhelmingly being traded on centralized exchanges. Nowhere is this more prevalent than on the crypto derivative and margin exchanges. People think that there are no real decentralized alternatives and even if there are, they require a PhD to operate. Well that was until dYdX opened their protocol. In the following chapters I'm going to share with you everything you need to know about dYdX. I'll also take you through the process of trading lending and borrowing on dYdX, as well as comparing it to some other apps. So what exactly is dYdX? Well, simply put it's a noncustodial decentralized crypto exchange or DEX. However unlike most other Dex's, here you can lend borrow and trade on margin. It's an open source trading protocol that was built on the Ethereum protocol and is powered by smart contracts. Given that it's non-custodial it means that no one else but you are in control of your private keys. Trading is done by connecting your Ethereum wallets to the exchange. No KYC, no limits, no questions. It was started back in 2017 and they raised over ten million dollars in seed funding from some well-known VC funds. It went live in May of 2019 and has grown considerably since then. There is currently just under 19 million dollars locked into the protocol and it's the 8th most used app. There has also been over 200 million dollars that has been traded on the protocol. So much growth for dYdX? Well, this comes down not only to its functionality but also its relative simplicity. An ideal mix for adoption from the broader crypto community. Let's take a look at some of these features starting with their primary MO; margin trading. Trading on the margin means increasing the size of your exposure to an asset through leverage. At the large centralized exchanges such as BitMEX the exchanges will loan you a position in an underlying crypto for only a small deposit, the margin. With a leverage position your gains and losses are magnified by the leverage factor. At a decentralized exchange, they will monitor your positions and if they deteriorate to a certain level then you will be liquidated. This is all done by the internal liquidation engine that these exchanges run. You can't see how these engines work and you don't know all the parameters that are used in those algorithms. At dYdX on the other hand the protocol is open-source. Fully auditable smart contracts adjust leverage ratios, free up margin and if need be, liquidate positions. You can see exactly how the protocol works in a fully transparent manner. Leverage at dYdX goes up to a maximum of five times or an equivalent margin position of 20%. You might be thinking that you can get up to 100 times over on BitMEX! Well, yes you can but do you really need 100 times leverage to be profitable? Let's not forget that leverage is a double-edged sword and you can lose just as quickly as you can gain. Is the benefit of trading with so much leverage worth the risk of trading against your preferred instrument? Five times leverage on a decentralized exchange is pretty good for most traders that know what they're doing. Also with lower leverage you have less risk of liquidation. Another really good feature that you have a dYdX is that you have two types of margin mechanisms you have isolated and then you have cross margin. Isolated margin is the mechanism that you're most likely to be quite familiar with. It's where you will isolate a particular amount of your funds as part of a trade with a specific leverage level. If there is a liquidation, the losses will be capped to your isolated position. But cross margin is something different. This utilizes all assets that you have in your account. It takes into account your combined position in your account when it is determining leverage and limits. There are a number of reasons as to why you may want to cross margin your trades. When it comes to trading pairs you have ETH-DAI, ETH-USDC and DAI-USDC. You can trade the difference between a centralized and decentralized stable coin. While leveraged trading is one of the selling points of dYdX, don't forget that's also a standard Dex. You can trade the above spot assets in the spot market.

The next feature that I want to share with you on dYdX is their lending feature. When you're lending your crypto out on dYdX, it's being lent out to other users on the platform and you are earning an interest on that deposit. This interest is earned on a continuous basis and is sent straight to your wallet. This is also relatively risk-free lending because the dYdX protocol ensures that the borrower's are over collateralized. What do I mean by that? Well, they have a collateralize a shin ratio that requires more crypto collateral than they have borrowed. This means that the market was to move quickly, there are enough funds to pay back the lenders. Another really great thing about dYdX and defy lending gaps like it is that there are no restrictions on the deposits. You can withdraw the funds lent whenever you like. The concept of a term deposit is alien in the crypto space. Given that this is a decentralized app there is no entity or intermediary that's controlling your lending. It's all managed through the use of transparent and decentralized smart contracts. This makes it quite different from other crypto lending platforms such as BlockFi or Nexo. The final primary feature of dYdX is the ability to borrow. Part of the reason that dYdX can operate a leverage Dex is because of the global lending pools facilitated by the protocol. These pools apply to a particular asset and are all operated by smart contracts. Supply and demand in these lending pools will determine what is called the utilization ratio. This is basically just the amount of funds that are utilized in the lending pool. So borrowed amount divided by supplied amount. This will have a direct impact on the interest rates that are being charged or earned. It's pretty clever. The same happens in traditional financial markets. Interest rates are seen as the cost of capital and they move according to how many people want to borrow a fixed portion of capital, versus those who want to supply it. That aside, borrowing on dYdX can be done up to a minimum collateralization ratio of 125%. Anything below this level and you cannot borrow any more crypto. Once that crypto hits 115%, your trade will be liquidated. This is in order to keep the trading pool solvent and keep the lenders that we talked about earlier hole. Those who are liquidated will have to pay a liquidation fee of 5%. This is done in order to make short borrowers keep their accounts well collateralized and firmly above the liquidation level.

Now you have a reasonable overview of the main features of the dYdX platform, but how can you use it? Well, it's actually pretty simple. So simple in fact, that you can even be forgiven for forgetting that it's a Dex. From the homepage of dYdX, you can select what you want to do trading, borrowing or lending. For me I'll discuss trading, so if you click on that, the main dYdX user interface it's pretty well laid out and looks much like your typical centralized cryptocurrency exchange. Here, you have your order forms, your order books, the buy/sell walls, charts open orders and positions. It's actually neat that they've included this trading view chart as this will allow some of you more technical traders to run your TA. You can also switch the chart here to view the market depth. In order to trade on dYdX or any decks for that matter, you have to connect your wallet to the dap. You can choose from any wallet here you can connect your ledger if you want but I will give you an example with Metamask. Once you wallet is connected, you'll need to approve the transaction on your device and you're ready to go. Like with any exchange, you'll need to deposit assets in your account. Given that you also have that lending component, you should note that the moment you deposit funds at dYdX, it will be placed into the lending pool and you will start earning interest. Give it some time for the network to process the transaction. Once it's fully confirmed and deposited into your account it will be reflected on your balance. Now you're ready to trade. Given that we're going to trade on margin, you have to select that one. Going to go long on ETH-USDC pair, you can choose the position size as well as the leverage. As mentioned your max is 5 but you can set a custom leverage limit if you want. When it comes to the Advanced Options, you can set your max slippage. This is basically the maximum amount that you will allow the price to fall and would still be happy executing the trade. If the price slips past this max slippage point, then the order will be cancelled. Regards to the expiry time point, dYdX trades are not perpetual. You can think of them more as regular futures that have expiry times. So once you reach expiry, the position will be automatically closed out. Once you're fully comfortable with the parameters and then you can place the order and it will go into the books. You'll be able to monitor your trade in the positions tab as well as your PNL. You also should keep an eye on that collateralization ratio. If you slip below the liquidation point, then you'll have your position closed and lose that liquidation fee. That's it. This is the margin trading feature.

Spot trading is much like the other standard Dex-s that you have seen. You will technically be swapping one crypto for another. You also have a lot more order functionality than you do on the margin trade. These include placing market orders, limits as well as stop orders. You can also select how long you'd like the order to remain open. It's time forced. So there is a bit more customization options around your orders here. Do note that if you have any leverage trades open, trading in the spot market will impact on your margin and in turn, collateralization ratio. So keep an eye on that. When it comes to lending on dYdX it's pretty simple. As mentioned, the moment that you deposit crypto onto the exchange, it will start earning interest. You can see those interest rates over in your balances tab at the top of the platform. Here you will have both the lend and the borrow rate on the various assets. You should also note that dYdX will take a 5% cut of all interest payments in order to fund an insurance pool to protect the protocol. This is already reflected in the rate. These rates are annual percentage rates but have paid continuously into your wallet. To complete this walkthrough, let's take a quick look at the borrowing feature. Here, at the top is the tab to borrow funds on dYdX. It's a pretty straightforward layout. On the left you have all your asset balances. Here you can repay outstanding balances and you can borrow new assets. Then in the center, you have all your outstanding borrows. Borrowing crypto is pretty simple. All you need to do is select the crypto that you want to borrow. Choose the amount you want to borrow as well as the crypto that you'll be depositing. For example if you want to borrow DAI and will be depositing ETH, you hit borrow DAI and confirm the transaction on your wallet. You will see the outstanding burrow show up in the center as well as all the interest rate that you'll be paying. That does it for the platform walkthrough so let's take a look at something I'm sure you want to know; the fees. Until recently it used to be free to trade on dYdX. You would sign a message to create an order in the book. When those orders were matched, dYdX submits a transaction to execute the match trades on chain. dYdX would have to pay the gas costs for this transaction. While this works smoothly with smaller trading volumes, as volume picked up this year so did gas costs. In February 2020 they had to fork out over at least $40,000 in gas fees in order to cover it. There was a change in March of this year where they announced that they would start charging fees in order to cover this cost. The fees that are being introduced will follow a standard maker take a model. Essentially those who are making markets and providing liquidity will get a lower rate than those who are taking it off the book. In the case of dYdX, makers will have zero fees and takers will be charged a few percentage points. Do note that there is a different take a feat for those who are trading less than 0.5 ETH. This is only logical as gas fees on transactions for small orders are just as large of those of larger orders. If we were to compare these fees to some of the larger exchanges such as Binance, the taker fee on orders above 0.5 ETH is slightly lower. Whereas its higher with orders below 0.5. Still pretty impressive for a decentralized exchange. In terms of any other fees that you could have to pay on dYdX, you have that liquidation fee that I mentioned and then if you allow the trade to expire, it will have to be traded. This trade carries a 1% price spread. All in all these fees are reasonable and are the cost of maintaining a secure and highly functional defy protocol.

dYdX has built a pretty simple client and trading API that will allow you to build trading BOTS. Much like you can build BOTS that interact with the large centralized exchanges, you can develop them here to trade on chain at dYdX. Except, when trading a dYdX you can place instant non-custodial trades. There are also a number of other benefits that can come with building bots at dYdX. Not only can you programmatically partake in the margin trading, but you can also run a liquidation bot. What is that? Well at dYdX you can also participate in the liquidation of under collateralized positions. Doing so, earns you that 5% liquidation fee that I mentioned before. If you're running a bot 24/7, you can basically scan for these under collateralized accounts and take advantage of them when the moment arises. dYdX have even provided the code for an open source liquidation bot. One of the final few things I want to look at is the competing d5 project dYdX is up against and how they compare. There are a number of other projects ranking higher in value locked than dYdX. The top three actually quite interesting called; maker, synthetics and compound. Maker is a decentralized autonomous organization or DAO, upon which the DAI stable coin is built. Since the issuance of DAI, it's become the most popular decentralized stable coin on the market. There was also recently an upgrade of the eco system to the multi collateral DAI. Basically this is also a lending protocol that has got a decentralized exchange feature as well. This is all done through the Oasis defy hub. While the lending and borrowing features are pretty straightforward the trading feature is left wanting. It's pretty basic and is way less advanced than dYdX's. Just after maker is synthetics, this was another really exciting project. It's a decentralized trading protocol that allows crypto traders to take positions on synthetic crypto assets. It does not only have to be crypto but it can also include a number of traditional asset classes. You can also trade inverse assets which would be similar to shorting a pair. There is no doubt more trading optionality than dYdX, you don't have margin trading. I also find that the trading interface is pretty basic when compared to that of dYdX. Of course some people find it's simplistic which is a plus. Finally, you have compound finance. This is a lending protocol that has also been making waves recently. It also has a pretty sizable lending pool. Apart from the size of the lending pool you also have much more optionality when it comes to lending and borrowing. Something that is pretty neat was the wrapped Bitcoin lending. This basically means that you can lend an ERC20 asset that tracks the price of Bitcoin. You can't trade on it like a Dex and you don't have margin trading optionality, so it won't really satisfy your needs there. I really like what the team is doing and they have built a pretty effective Dify dap. It's pretty easy to use for most crypto traders used to the large centralized exchanges. The simplicity does not come at the cost of reduced functionality. Lending, margin trading, borrowing and liquidation are all part of the dYdX package. The recent introduction of trading fees may disappoint some of the earlier traders on the protocol but it was always expected. Upgrades take time and developers got to eat. I would recommend giving dYdX a try if you haven't already. Of course be sure to manage your risk and never trade lend or borrow more than you can afford. If you are interested to sign up or want to look at the platform you can find it at https://dydx.exchange/

When it comes to day trading crypto there are such an amazing opportunities out there. But there is one major problem. Crypto markets never sleep and most people need to catch sleep from time to time. That leads to many traders going to bed and waking up only to discover they missed out on a huge market move and an amazing trading opportunity. This isn't a problem for some traders. Why is that? Well, it's because some use crypto trading BOTS. In the following chapters I'll explain what crypto trading bots are. I will also go over the pros and cons of using them and compare the top trading BOTS side-by-side. So what are crypto trading bots? Well, they are computer programs that trade on your behalf with a given set of instructions or rule criteria to act on. So that might be something like buy X amount of Bitcoin if a certain price target is hit. Once that rule criteria is met, then the bots will automatically execute the trade you wanted. What this means is that in order to use a crypto trading bot, you will need to connect it to a crypto exchange account using something known as an API or application program interface. Basically that API gives your trading BOTS the ability to place trades programmatically at the exchange. The result is that you can execute trades in your sleep. You're essentially handing over access to your exchange account to a computer program. What happens if there is compromised code in the bot or the company that made the crypto BOTS turn out to be scammers? These are all very real concerns that you must be aware of. Are the machines going to take over your Binance account? Well not exactly. The good news is that you can set permissions for exchange API's. You can determine what particular API keys have the ability to do in your account. So for the crypto trading BOT, you can set the ability to only write orders buy or sell but not to initiate a withdrawal. Most likely a good idea. You can also limit IP addresses too. What that means is that any instructions must come from your own IP address which is a neat way to protect yourself against a scammy crypto trading bot. So now that you know what a trading bot is I want to go over the pros and cons of using them and give you some cold hard truths. One major Pro is that these BOTS enable you to trade 24/7 and execute trades in your sleep. That means you'll never miss out on the another trading opportunity ever again. Also trading BOTS help take the emotion out of trading. You are simply setting the rule criteria or instructions in the bot and leaving those trades to execute if your criteria are met. That means you should be less susceptible to FOMO or panic selling. Another benefit of using bots is that they allow you to back test your trading strategy. What that means is that a bot can take that strategy you're using and apply it to all that historical crypto price data and tell you how successful it is. Finally trading bots simplify trading. But they are pretty expensive. Given that a crypto trading bot can access and simultaneously carry out multiple trades across multiple different exchanges you only need a laptop to be trading. Still not all is well when it comes to crypto trading BOTS. I'm going to have to be straight up on the cons. Many people seem to be under the illusion that trading BOTS are some form of magical money printing machine. Get one, switch it, on and you make money all day long. Sorry but that's not the case at all. With a bot you have to constantly tweak your trading strategy. That is work and it is certainly not a set and forget it money printer. Another con for crypto BOTS is that there are a bunch of scams out there. Even if you find a legitimate one some are so poorly coded that it's going to be impossible for you to execute a single profitable trade. Therefore you need to be really careful with crypto trading BOTS. If it sounds too good to be true then it probably is. I will list a few trading BOTS shortly, but if you choose to use a different trading BOTS that's completely fine. It's always good to assess your options but if you see trading BOTS claiming to guarantee returns for low one-off pricing, please run for the hills. More than likely it's a scam. Another thing many people do not realize is that crypto BOTS need to be monitored. Do not expect to switch on a crypto trading bot and be laughing all the way to the bank. The market is cyclical. Trends come and go all the time. Basically a bot is not a substitute for being a smart trader. To use them, you will need to keep your funds on an exchange. There are a lot of highly reputable and secure exchanges out there but hacks do happen. With all that said, in the following chapters I will list some of the best and most well-known crypto trading bots.

TradeSanta is cloud-based BOT and has a solid reputation with over 45,000 active users 14,000 active trading BOTS and 1.8 million completed trades. However I do want to give you a fair warning. It may take you a while to get used to some of the functionality. When it comes to features, TradeSanta offers a long bot template to use when you expect a crypto asset to rise in price, a short bot template when you think it will fall and a custom template which gives you the freedom to leverage the full functionality of the bot. In addition to all that TradeSanta offers you a excess of technical indicators to digest. These include things like Bollinger signals, trade filters and volume filters. Another neat feature that is great is the real-time tracking, which enables you to monitor the bots progress on-the-go with transparent analytics and telegram notifications. TradeSanta has also got an iOS and Android app. When it comes to exchanges, TradeSanta supports HitBTC, Binance, BitMEX, Houbi, OKEX, Bitfinex and BITtrex too. In terms of pricing, the good news is that TradeSanta offers a 5 day free trial. So you can jump in there and play around with the bot to see if it's worth your hard-earned money. After that you can use the free version which gives you access to just two bots and has a maximum monthly volume limit of $3,000. On top of all that, you'll get access to an unlimited number of trading pairs, all TradeSanta strategies, telegram notifications and general customer support. The basic plan gives you access to everything the minimum plan offers, while unlocking access to up to 49 BOTS and allowing you to run an unlimited amount of trade volume through the bot. That will set you back $14 a month. This is the plan I recommend for most people who choose to opt for TradeSanta. However you can upgrade to the hit BTC promo plan for another $7 per month. This gives you everything in the basic plan plus 0% trading fees on HitBTC. Some might say that's a valuable benefit but I'm not the biggest fan of HitBTC. The top pay plan on TradeSanta basically gives you access to everything the basic plan does, plus the 0% in trading fees on HitBTC and access to an unlimited number of bots. That will set you back to $70 per month. Honestly I doubt any of you will really need to shell out $70 a month. So what are the pros and cons of TradeSanta. Well you should certainly have this bot on your short list if you want lots of automated trading options and are looking for an intuitive interface and reliable security measures. The bot is also well suited to beginners dipping their toes into the crypto bot waters. Needless to say, automating your crypto trading with such a tool is going to give you loads of time and there is a super active trading community, to meet like-minded traders too. Still, there are drawbacks. It lacks support for some of the major high liquidity exchanges like Kraken and KuCoin and doesn't support any decentralized exchanges. It's also not really suitable for taking advantage of arbitrage opportunities and is not open source. Who is **TradeSanta** for? Well, in my opinion this bot is ideal for any crypto day trader that's not interested in futures trading and envisions that they will take crypto bots seriously. It's also beginner friendly, so if you're new to the world of crypto bots then this is a great place to start. To learn more about TradeSanta, please visit their website at https://tradesanta.com/en

Shrimpy is a social portfolio management tool and crypto trading platform that bursts onto the scene in 2018 and quickly gained a ton of popularity in the trading community. The value proposition was simple. Provide as many top-of-the-line trading tools for the lowest price possible. That's why they offer a good range of services for free. What's important to note is that Shrimpy is not designed for signals or indicators. So it's not the best tool for day traders. Instead it is a longer-term portfolio management tool which automates things like portfolio rebalancing, dollar cost averaging, and stop losses. That approach is perfect for anyone that wants to take a top-level view of their portfolio and wishes to automate the management of that. Unlike other trading bots that provide almost every possible indicator, signal and stat, Shrimpy eliminates that complexity by focusing only on core long-term trading strategies. That makes things super easy for beginners and this is also why Shrimpy is normally the first crypto trading bot I recommend to friends interested in this bots. Another important feature is their social portfolio management. This enables you to take a bit of a backseat when it comes to managing your funds and allows you to select other traders to manage your portfolio for you. You can also select the best traders on the platform and get a copy of their trading strategy without, copy trading them. That's a great learning tool and you should definitely check out. Also Shrimpy offers a pretty powerful back testing tool. So if you have that ultimate trading strategy that you want to put to the test, then you can do so right here. Right now Shrimpy doesn't have a mobile app. If that's important to you then you should certainly weigh up other options. The Shrimpy crypto trading bot is also supported on a ton of different exchanges such as KuCoin, Binance, Coinbase, GEMENI, OKEX, Bitfinex, Poloniex, BITtrex, BitMart and Huobi Global. What's the cost of all this? Well Shrimpie offers a pretty extensive free plan that allows you to link unlimited exchanges to monitor your portfolio performances, blacklist assets gives you access to an asset balance tracker and more. However if you want to automate that portfolio management back test those trading strategies or use Shrimpie social trading features, then you'll need to opt for a paid plan. That will set you back just $13 per month if you opt for the annual plan or $19 per month if you want to pay monthly. Additionally, Shrimpie does offer an enterprise plan too. So what are the benefits and drawbacks of Shrimpie? Well they offer a lot of features entirely for free and the subscription fees are quite reasonable. If you are a crypto HODLer and want to automate things like portfolio rebalancing and dollar cost averaging, then Shrimpie is going to save you so much time. The social trading feature is also ideal for anyone that wants to leverage the knowledge of top crypto traders that do nothing but eat, sleep, trade and repeat. In terms of drawbacks ,Shrimpie is not open sourced so you're going to have to trust the thousands of people using it that the code is good. Also there's no mobile app which could be a deal breaker for some. Finally, Shrimpie does not provide the functionality that most active day traders will need. If that's you then there are certainly better options out there coming up in the following chapters. In my opinion Shrimpie is a top option for long term crypto holders who want to automate that portfolio management or want to copy trade some of the best traders in the space. To learn more about Shrimpie, please visit their website at https://www.shrimpy.io/

The next crypto bot on my list is called Gunbot. Gunbot also known as Gun-T. It's a pretty popular crypto bot that is compatible with Mac, Windows and Linux so you can run it on practically any computer. When it comes to features Gunbot comes with numerous inbuilt trading strategies that include the likes of step game, gain and ping pong. Another cool thing is that you can customize your trading strategies in Gunbot and the bot will execute those trades for you. When it comes to mobile support Gunbot is pretty well mobile optimized. Gunbot also supports a ton of top-tier exchanges like Coinbase Pro and margin trading on BITmex, Kraken and OKEX. What's the pricing for Gunbot? Well this one differs from the rest which have a subscription-based model. Instead Gunbot charges a one-time license fee. The starter pack is 0.02 Bitcoin. However you'll only be able to use Gunbot to trade on one supporters exchange and access free trading strategies. Gunbot standard offers access to all trading strategies, but you will still only be able to use the bot on one exchange. That will set you back 0.05 Bitcoin. Gunbot Pro is where things start really heating up in the pricing stakes it will set you back 0.075 Bitcoin but you will be able to use the bot on three exchanges and you'll get access to trading strategy back testing too. The bot also offers a wide range of add-ons and upgrades as well. In terms of pros and cons, I really like the variety of trading strategies on offer at Gunbot. It's also easy to use and supports exchanges like Coinbase Pro but the downside is that Gunbot feels relatively expensive with its one-off fee structure. Who is Gunbot for? Basically anyone who wants a beginner friendly crypto trading bot that intends to be trading crypto seriously for a long time. To learn more about Gunbot, please visit their website at https://www.gunbot.com/

Next crypto bot on my list is called Crypto Hopper. Crypto Hopper provides expert trading tools without the need for coding skills. If you are into more advanced trading stuff like market making and exchange arbitrage, then this bot has you covered. The Crypto Hopper marketplace also boasts a plethora of trading templates, strategies and signals to choose from. These signals allow you to subscribe to professional analysts around the world and Crypto Hopper uses these signals to trade. But be warned that not everything in the marketplace is free. If you want to access your trading bot on the go, the good news is that there is an Android and iOS app. When it comes to crypto exchange support, Crypto Hopper integrates with KuCoin, Binance, Coinbase, OKEX, Bitfinex, Poloniex, BITtrex, HitBTC Kraken and Huobi Global. In terms of cost, Crypto Hopper offers a 7-day free trial. The basic pan will set you back 16 dollars per month and is ideal for more day traders. If you're into exchange arbitrage then you'll be paying $41 per month and the market making license is 83 dollars per month. What are the pros and cons of this bot? Well on the pro side it is easy to setup keenly priced. The marketplace is great and there is good coin and exchange support. If I was to have one gripe it would be that I cannot see who is behind the bot.

Transparency goes a long way in crypto. Who can benefit from Crypto Hopper? Well honestly almost anyone that is interested in using a pro level crypto bot at a reasonable price. To learn more about Crypto Hopper, please visit their website at https://www.cryptohopper.com/

My number one trading bot is called 3commas. What you need to know is that this is one of the most popular BOTS out there with over 140,000 users and 65 million dollars in trade volume every day. It has a super intuitive interface packed full of detailed analytics and a ton of functions. The bot also enables you to set stop loss and take profit targets and craft your own trading strategies. Personally I find 3commas smart trading functionality particularly useful. For example you might want to buy Ethereum with Bitcoin. But on some exchanges when you make an audit you need to decide if you want to set a take profit, or a stop loss. You cannot always set both and that's pretty inconvenient. But with 3commas that is something you can do as well as set trailing stop losses easily and quickly. That means, if the market jumps up 5% then the trailing stop loss raises your stop-loss by 5%. Some exchanges do allow you to set take profit levels and stop losses at the same time but if that trading pair you want to trade isn't there, then you don't have to pass up that opportunity anymore. On top of all that 3commas offers back testing, dollar cost averaging BOTS, a ton of different trading tools, a traders diary to keep all your trades in one place and a highly developed signals marketplace which allows you to mimic and automate the trades given by the top signals providers. That means you can follow them signals and let the bot do the hard work. 3commas has not forgotten about mobile users too. Just hit that App Store and you will see that the bot supports all sorts of major exchanges such as KuCoin, Binance, Binance DEX, Binance Futures, BitStamp,EXMO, YoBit, GateIO, CEX.io Coinbase Pro, OKEX, Bitfinex, Poloniex, BITtrex, HitBTC Kraken and Huobi Global. Cost wise, 3commas offers a free three day trial and prices range from anywhere between $14,50 per month and $49 50. If you are not into futures trading then the plan for $25 is what you want. Onto the pros and cons, in my opinion 3commas has one of the best interfaces out there. It's got copy trading supports a ton of exchanges and offers that sweet signals marketplace. On top of all that I cannot stress how useful that smart trading feature is. 3commas is probably not the best pick for inexperienced traders. So if you're an experienced trader looking for all the bells and whistles, you need look no further than 3commas. As mentioned before one drawback of using these bots is having to keep your funds on an exchange. Which of course does have its risks but there is no getting away from that if you want to use them. So if you're going to be running trading bots then I do recommend that you split your funds across more than one exchange. These bots support multiple exchanges which makes it easier to spread that risk. Also if you're going to be using a bot that I haven't mentioned before, make sure that you do your research and extra suspicious of any bots that promise returns. There have been a number of instances in the past where API Keys have been phished in order to conduct malicious trades so be aware of that. In the end crypto trading BOTS definitely won't make you a millionaire, but if used correctly they can equip you with the tools to improve your trading game. To learn more about 3commas, please visit their website at https://3commas.io/

Imagine that your mate just told you about this super-hot hidden gem of a crypto that's about to 1,000 times and take you to the moon. He seems convinced and has you on the edge. You're training accounts is open and ready to buy some. But how do you know that you're not about to buy a sh*tcoin? Indeed, how do you even know what a sh*tcoin looks like? In the following chapters I'm going to tell you exactly what to look for, some key metrics signals and red flags that should have you running for the hills. I'll also be letting you know about some top tools that I use to screen out these bad apples while doing my due diligence. Before I dive in I want to lay some groundwork before we start this analysis. I know some people can get testy when you claim that their moon sh*tcoin is a junk and some of these bag holders can be pretty emotional. So I need to point out that if a coin or token meets one of my sh*tcoin criteria, this does not mean that they should be immediately dismissed. Those coins that should be viewed with suspicion are those that meet many of these criteria. Indeed there are many projects that may take one or two boxes but could still be pretty good for the long term model. So at the end of the day you have to decide on where you sh*tcoin alert will be triggered. With that out of the way, let's start with the sh*tcoin sitting. I'm going to start with a top-down approach. This saves you time before you start digging into the weeds of the project itself. The first thing I tend to look at is also one of the most obvious and that is exchange listings. Simply you can tell a lot about a project by which exchanges their token trades, or if it has much exchange support at all. Why is this? Well quite simply most reputable exchanges don't want to be associated with coins that they deem to be useless. By that I mean they don't want to have a lot of angry traders coming to them because they lost nearly all their money on some vapourware project. Moreover it also creates certain problems for you buying the cryptocurrency. How can you feel really comfortable using some exchange that you've never really heard of just to buy that rare altcoin someone flagged? So if you're analyzing some low market cap old coin and you see that there is very little exchange support that should be a concern. It should also be a real concern if it's listed on some exchanges that are known to be on the dodgy end of the spectrum. I can't go over all of the shady exchanges but there are a number of sites that can conglomerate this data. You can use Coinmarketcap but you should be still skeptical of trusting their exchange rankings. Still, there are some decent alternatives. One of those go-to sites for me is called CoinGecko. Much like CMC, this is a another market cap aggregation tool. But what I'm really interested in is their exchange rating tools. Here you can see a list of the top exchanges and their trust score. If you're looking into an exchange that lists a coin you're considering, then you can just search for it here. Then you'll be given the trust score and you can make a judgement on that. Of course you should not take the CoinGecko trust ranking as some Bible. You could also just take a look at what other users have said about the exchange online. Dodgy exchanges do eventually get called out. To check out CoinGecko, please visit the site at https://www.coingecko.com/en Or, if you want to take a look at Coinmarketcap, please visit https://coinmarketcap.com/

Moving on, assuming that the coin is listed on an exchange that is relatively reputable, you need to make sure that it is actually being traded. The volume and liquidity of a token is important to study. Not only can it give you a broader indication of interest, but it will also help you determine whether you will be able to easily buy or sell the cryptocurrency yourself. Let's start off with the volume. You can easily see this data on sites like Coinmarketcap or CoinGecko now the trading volume of a cryptocurrency should not be viewed as an absolute number but rather as a proportion of the market cap of the coin itself. Any coin that has a 24-hour trading volume that is less than 5% is considered quite low. But even if the volume tends to be healthy for 24-hour period, this could be a trick. That's because volume can easily be artificially manipulated this is especially the case for those dodgy projects that want to make their trading appear active. The term is wash trading and it's dodgy. Trying to spot wash trading can be quite difficult. There are a number of order book red flags that you should be looking out for. I have explained washtrading in detail in my other book called Bitcoin and Cryptocurrency Trading:Must have tools, Best Exchanges and Trading Strategies. You can also use another quick tool over at CoinGecko.

You can click on the coin in question and you can select the market section. This gives you an overview of the liquidity, across all the exchanges where it's listed. You can just take a look at that trust score column to get an idea of whether the trading pair has decent enough liquidity. If most of the pairs of the coin on CoinGecko appear to have low liquidity, then it could be a sign of a low interest aldcoin, not something you want to buy. That does it for some of the coin market metrics, so now let's take a look at the development activity.

If the project appears to be relatively well supported with decent liquidity, then you're going to want to take a closer look at its development. Something that I always do when analyzing a project is to take a look at their public code repositories; their github or get labs. If their code is not public, that could be a red flag. Some projects developing private repositories before pushing live, but you cannot verify this. Moreover, cryptocurrency and blockchain technology is about transparency. All of the most successful crypto projects have open source code. If they do make their code public in their reps, then you'll want to observe how much has been done over the past few months. You don't have to be a developer to do this. You just want to see that there has been a regular stream of commits and discussions. If it's unproductive and thin with virtually no activity, then that should set some alarm bells ringing. What are the developers been doing in the past few months? While we're on the notion of activity you'll also want to take a look at whether the project has been active in other spheres. Do they have a blog and is the team keeping the community updated? What about some of their social channels? Do they update their Twitter regularly and can you see life over there? There needs to be a balance. No one wants to see a meaningless tweets for the sake of tweeting. An announcement of an upcoming announcement, but if the team has not found anything useful to mention in the past few weeks maybe they're not doing anything useful. Speaking of the team, here's a great segue into my next subject to explore. A project can have all the right ideas an amazing use case and great community support, but if the team is sketchy you can be pretty sure that that will feed into the project. Sketchy is a pretty broad term that encompasses a number of different factors. Firstly, are the team who they claim to be? Can you confirm their credentials on their social platforms like LinkedIn? Have they been involved in any questionable projects in the past? How long have they been involved in the blockchain space and is their background relevant for the project? Relevance is also a bit more nuanced but you can be a fair judge of this. If the whole team is made up of X marketing folk who know how to type, then I'm a bit less inclined to support it. In the world of crypto projects cutting-edge tech is what gets you above the crown. If most of the team members are not technical then how can we be sure they know what to develop. Also if there's one thing that we've seen in the crypto space so far, a good marketing strategy can push vaporware projects to astronomical highs. The simple rule of thumb is this. If these guys were pitching for an investment in their seed ground startup, would you feel comfortable investing in it?

Let's assume that the crypto has managed to pass most of your high-level criteria it's time to dig a little deeper into the project itself. The first thing that you need to ask yourself when looking at the project value proposal is; does this actually need a token or cryptocurrency? There are numerous examples of projects that have developed a cryptocurrency for something that really did not need one at all. Let's not forget that the future value of a utility token will come from its actual use. There are projects that I've seen that have developed a cryptocurrency for dentists, farmers or sports stars. This question of token utility becomes even more relevant for those projects that have completed ICOs or built on EtherEum. If you really need people to transact in your network why can't they just use ETH? Why do they need to use your token? Being able to stake on the network is not a legitimate use case. Why should I expect any sort of price appreciation and value from your token when I can just buy a Ethereum and capture all the additional value generated from network use. So if a project has a token or coin just for the sake of it, you have to wonder whether it could ever face mass adoption and be worth a lot more in the future. Speaking of use cases, this then brings us onto the topic of business development. At the end of the day a theoretical use case is nothing unless it's been put into practice. You need to take a look into the integrations and partnerships that the project is either engaged with, or working on. This could give you a sense of how they envision the token so eventually being used or mass adopted. Are these partnerships meaningful or are they merely a partnership for partnerships sake? A simple collaboration, or memorandum of understanding? Something that's concrete, or nothing more than a simple meeting. I have seen far too many projects that overhype a partnership that is either completely false or extremely misleading. There have been examples of cases where the other side of the arrangement needed to come out and further clarify the exact nature of the partnership. Of course a project and cryptocurrency may still be in it's relatively early stages and businesses or developers may not have started integrating yet. That's totally understandable. But do they have a strategy to increase adoption? Have they outlined a broader commercialization strategy? Far too often teams will claim that their blockchain project and cryptocurrency could disrupt an industry, but they don't have the first clue about how they're going to do it. This just shows that they were never really all too serious about the adoption and the more driven by hope. So make sure that they have some plan on this front. Assuming that the project has been around for some time then you have a lot more information to go with to help inform your opinion. This is where track records speak volumes. So you need to ask yourself if the project has some consistency in its vision. Those projects often change their focus and reinvent themselves every single year, almost definitely wants to watch out for. If their previous core use case is no longer a strong one what is to say their new one is any better? Moreover if they could not execute on their previous strategy why should you have any confidence that they're able to do it with the new vision. I have seen it all. Projects that started out as a development blockchain that would be an Ethereum killer then switching their focus to blockchain storage or supply chain tracking. Completely flipping the script as if that is supposed to inspire any confidence. Projects like V-chain or Chain-link had one vision strategy and focus that has defined them from the beginning; consistency. The same can't be said about projects like Factom for instance who constantly shifted the goalposts and eventually ran out of funds. They recently filed for chapter 11 bankruptcy protection. Also while we're on the subject of consistency, this is not just about the broader vision and use cases. It's also around its development goals and roadmap. Do they often missed milestones and have some of these proposed milestones just vanish from the ether? Sometimes I wonder if some development teams even know that an old roadmap can easily be pulled up and analyzed for progress. Reading over their old road maps and white paper is an important point of the analysis, at least at a glance. These initial documents can help me to determine how things have changed. If you read their latest roadmap and they have really grand visions, you can place that in the right context when viewing their old ones. While we're on track record, there is something else that you can observe for all those projects that raised an ICO and that is how that money is being spent. Of course, you might find that the team isn't tell you what they're spending their money on. Well, that should kind of answer the question. Most legitimate projects with a foundation will have detailed reports as to where the funds are being allocated and what they're being spent on. If no such disclosures exists then it's an immediate red flag. If they don't want you to know what the funds are being spent on. well there must be a reason. Then for those projects that do disclose this, you need to ask yourself whether it falls in line with their white paper budget allocation or whether it is at all justified. Let me give you a few examples to illustrate this. For example a project called Sirin labs raised a total of 157 million dollars in an ICO back in 2017. The goal was to develop a blockchain phone. They issued their own token in the ICO which of course asks the question; was a token even needed? The CEO have spent a fortune to get a Messy sponsorship of their phone. It seemed to be all good until you realized that the phone itself, well, no one really wanted to buy it. Sirin labs burned through all of those ICO funds pretty quickly to the extent that they had to lay off half of some of their workforce. A 157 million dollars gone. What did they spend those funds on? Well, no one really knows. I don't mean to take stabs at these projects. Just wanted to give you guys some concrete example of irresponsible spending of project funds.

Speaking of irresponsible allocation of funds to more metrics that I want to mention are the page shell factor and sock puppet index. Those crypto projects that have to rely on page shells to pump their coin or token should be view with immense suspicion. Why should they feel the need to create an artificial perception of demand? Does that mean that there is no real organic interest in the project? So what do these shells and sock puppets look like? Well they could range from a very well-known influencer all the way down to those individuals who always spam and comments on forums and other platforms with shameless project plugs. When it comes to the latter, these are either basic user accounts or merely bot farms that spread the project around. It just screams of desperation and it is a major turnoff. Don't get me wrong, projects are perfectly entitled to pay for coverage from influencers and other alternative media channels. However these should be fully disclosed and transparent. Honesty is the best policy. And those projects that try to manipulate the narrative, should be on your sh*tcoin shortlist. As mentioned just because a crypto meets one or even two of these criteria does not necessarily imply that it should be avoided. There could realistically be a situation with a coin that's just new to the market and with very limited exchange support and volume, but is singing all the right tunes when it comes to the other criteria. Indeed newer and relatively less hyped projects may not have the coverage of established altcoins, but they could still be hidden gems. So when using these criteria, it's important to view it holistically. I also encourage you not to use the term "scam" too liberally. Just because a coin is junk, does not mean that it's a scam. It does not mean that the developers or creators have any malicious intent. It just means that they've developed a cryptocurrency that is not valuable, unique or in demand for anyone else. And that is not a crypto you want to hold.

With over a million downloads, it's safe to say that the crypto.com app has been taking the world by storm. What's all the fuss about and should you bother giving it a try? Well, in the following chapters I'm going to go over everything that the crypto.com app has to offer. All that is to help you decide if it's the right choice for you. The first thing I want to talk about is the apps integrated multi crypto and Fiat wallets. You can find this crypto wallet in the app by opening up the home screen and clicking the little lion at the bottom of the screen. Then just tap the wallet tile and you'll be in the crypto wallet section of the app. Here you can store over 80 different cryptos. That's a lot of coins and chances are that the cryptos you want to store will be supported here. Like any other crypto wallet, you can send or receive crypto. You can do that by clicking on the transfer button. Click deposit, if you want to send crypto to your crypto.com wallet. Then choose the crypto currency you want to deposit. Then you'll see your crypto wallet address to send to. When it comes to withdrawals, there are two major things I need to be upfront about. The first is that there is a fee to withdraw to non crypto.com wallets. The problem is that there is no functionality to adjust the transaction speed and fee. Instead it's set at a flat rate and there is nothing you can do about it. For Bitcoin this is set at 0.0003 Bitcoin which is just under 5 dollars. That's not really good. How to actually withdraw from the crypto.com app? Well, in that crypto wallet section you'll need to hit that transfer button and click that withdraw button. Then select the type of wallet do you want to withdraw to. You'll then be asked to whitelist the wallet address you want to withdraw to. Click the little plus sign in the top right corner then just select the crypto you want to withdraw and input that address. Once done you'll get an email from crypto.com asking you to confirm and authorize that wallet address. You'll then be able to withdraw to that whitelist as well as address and all you need do is key in the withdrawal amount and click on withdraw. Moving on, the crypto.com also has a Fiat wallet too. This allows you to buy crypto with a bank account. Up to 21 different fiat currencies are supported but some of those might be restricted depending on what country you're based in. So if you're searching for an alternative way to get into crypto currency, then you can do that with the crypto.com app. But what about the fees? Well, the good news is that crypto.com doesn't charge you a fee for deposits all withdrawals using Swift bank transfers to and from the app. The bad news is that your bank may charge you between 6 to 40 dollars for a transaction. But what other features does this app have? "Crypto earn" essentially allows you to lend out your crypto on the app and earn interest. Bear in mind that your typical bank account pays out less than 1% interest per year. It's pretty easy to see why so many people are flocking to crypto earn, when you can get an annual interest rate as high as 18%. What's important to note is that the interest rate for supplying crypto on the app varies according to the crypto currency you supply, the lending term and if you have 500 MCO state or not. 500 MCO is not cheap and will set you back over 2500 dollars. However if you have that stake within the app you'll get an additional interest bonus of 2% on fixed term deposits. So to get that 18 interests you'll need to have those MCO tokens state within the app. The other thing to be aware of is that interest rates vary according to the crypto asset you're supplying. With stable coins you can get up to 12% interest. 18% if you supply CRO and you can get up to 8% with other assets. So if you're interested in getting the highest interest possible then you better go with CRO. the final variable is the length of the staking term. the crypto.com app gives you three different options. tlexible staking is naturally the most flexible plan. it provides a low risk saving solution that allows you to test out the waters and withdraw your coins at any point with no penalty fees. lock your coins up for one month and you'll be rewarded with more interest and you'll get the maximum interest rate if you commit that crypto to be locked up for three months. On top of all that you'll get an additional 2% bolted on if you have 500 MCO state. So that's how you get up to 18% max interest here and one of the reasons why you might want to stock up on some CRO. All this sounds amazing however you should know that MCO and CRO are both crypto currencies issued by crypto.com. Another cool feature of this app is the ability to get an instant crypto loan, using the crypto credit service. Applying for a conventional loan you'll know that it requires a ton of paperwork and that it's extremely slow. With crypto credit, there are no annoying credit checks at all, no boring forms to fill in, and it's instant. So what wizardry is this? Well these loans are over collateralized loans where you can supply Bitcoin, Ethereum XRP or Litecoin as collateral and get 50% of its US dollar value in stable coins like Paxos, Tether USD coin and Tru USD in return. Interest rates start at 12% per year. But you can drop that down to 8% if you're staking 500 MCO coins. Another thing you need to know is that the credit duration is 12 months. Before you jump right into that crypto lending it's important to understand how over collateralized loans work before you consider using them. These types of loans are similar to getting a loan from your local pawnbroker. That's where you take an item like a car, jewellery or pretty much anything of value to the pawnbrokers and receive a loan based on the value of the item. The pawnbroker might lend you 50% of the value of the item, charge you interest and if you miss your repayments, they might sell your item to recoup the value of the loan. As pawn brokers always lend you less than the value you're putting up for collateral, the loans they provide are always over collateralized. Crypto credit in the crypto.com app works in a pretty similar way. You bring that crypto collateral which is then locked up and you receive 50% of that collateral value in stable coins. We all know that crypto markets can be volatile so it's important to be aware that if the market price of your collateral falls too much, then you'll have your crypto liquidated by crypto.com to cover the value of the loan. It's very much like a pawnbroker selling an item to cover the cost of the loan that's gone south. In other words if the crypto price moves against you by 50%, then you could lose the rights to that crypto you've supply and be left hodling stable coins. The next app feature I want to talk about is called "crypto pay" and that's all about buying stuff with crypto. One cool thing you can do here is buy gift cards for over three hundred bands with Bitcoin, Ethereum CRO, XRP and Litecoin. If that wasn't good enough, you can also get up to 10% cashback if you use CRO to buy them. The exact level of cashback depends on a few factors including what type of gift card you buy, if you have an active fixed deposit term of greater than 10000 CRO or if you've staked more than 10000 CRO in the crypto.com exchange. So if most of your money in crypto, you might find things like supermarket gift cards particularly useful. That's all the more sweet up when you're getting 5% cash back rewards too. Crypto pay also includes something called airtime, which allows you to top-up your mobile phone, using crypto or if you're feeling generous your friends. The final thing that crypto pay has to offer is a scanner to allow you to spend your crypto at any supported store. Just scan that QR code and you'll be making that crypto payment in no time. Another neat feature of the app is its crypto tracking function. Most people do not know this but if you click the account button and hit "pie chart" in the top left-hand corner, then you'll get a nice visual breakdown of all the coins you hold on the app. A pretty cool way to track your portfolio. If you want to make sure you keep your finger on the pulse of the crypto markets then this app also offers a handy alternative to Coinmarketcap and gives you all that price data for the top crypto currencies. You can also click into different coins to see price graphs and more detailed stats. Pretty useful. Another great feature here is the price alert function. Hit that Bell for any cryptocurrency and you'll get push notifications if there are any major price movements. That means you'll be the first to know if there is a price break out that you want to trade. To learn more about the app, please visit their website at https://crypto.com/en/index.html

Now it's time to talk about the main reason why most people use the crypto.com app. That would be getting a crypto.com card. The first thing to know here is that you can only get your hands on one of these crypto cards if you're based in the US, UK, Europe, Canada or Singapore. The second is that they support Bitcoin, Ethereum, Litecoin, XRP and MCO. So if you like the idea of being able to spend any of those cryptos using a Visa card, then this is going to be for you. The key question is which one should you choose? There are five different card tiers and if you're interested in knowing all the details about every card then check out their site within the card Compare tier list here: https://crypto.com/en/cards.html

However I'm going to go over my top two card picks. After all I don't think many people would be that interested in learning about the black obsidian card which will set you back over a quarter of a million dollars to get. Honestly I think the crypto.com blue card is a no-brainer for anyone in crypto. It's completely free and I cannot see what anyone has to lose by ordering one. In terms of perks, you're looking at 1% in crypto cash back on all purchases. One thing to note here is that all cash back is paid in MCO coin. Not that big a deal seems it's the top 100 cryptocurrency with a ton of trade volume and supported by numerous exchanges. So what else can you get with this card? Well, you can withdraw up to $200 per month from an ATM for free. However be aware that you'll be charged 2% for cash withdrawals over that amount. Pretty ideal for a casual crypto card user. Another thing that's great is that if you manage to go abroad you can access interbank exchange rates with a monthly exchange limit of $2000. I don't know about you but whenever I go on vacation I shop around for ages trying desperately to get the best exchange rate. That's a thing of the past with this card is that interbank rate is pretty much going to be the best rate you'll ever get. Here is my favorite crypto card called the crypto.com Ruby card. To get it, you'll have to stake 50 MCO tokens in the crypto.com app. This is just over $250. The important thing to know is that these tokens are only staked and you can get them back later. So it's a very different situation to annual card fees. With that barrier to entry what do you get? Well, right off the bat your crypto cash back is doubled to 2%. That's honestly more than what Amex used to give back in the day for a ludicrously expensive credit card. You'll also get a free Spotify subscription too. That rebate is paid into your crypto.com wallet in MCO. What Spotify worth? Well in the US this will set your rack around $9.99 a month. So in a year you can expect around 120 dollars' worth of value from that free

Spotify subscription alone. When it comes to maximizing those cash back rewards, here's my little secret. I personally try and run every possible transaction through this card to really take full advantage of those rewards. So if you easily spend $1,000 a month on just surviving, then you could have 12,000 dollars in transactions running through the card a year, which equates to about two hundred and forty dollars in crypto cash back. All that for simply choosing to leave that fiat card at home. Another thing I really like about this card is that it's made out of metal. There seems to be something super alluring when you slap down a metal credit card to pay that bill. What I can almost guarantee is that heads will turn if you flex that metal card. Free ATM withdrawal limits on this card are raised to $400 month and you also get access to 4000 dollars' worth of interbank exchange rates per month. So what's the value summary for the Ruby card? In the year you'll get 120 dollars in value from that for Spotify subscription, 2% in crypto cash back and that metal Visa Card. After running that through the value calculator I come to the sum of 360 dollars in value. Not too bad if you ask me.

The last app feature is the trading function. You can access that on the home screen by clicking the trade button. Selecting buy or sell, choosing the crypto you want to trade and execute in that order. It's honestly, that simple. However I do want to share a few closing thoughts. The first thing I want to address is whether crypto.com is legit. I'll be honest with you. There are some out there that believe that crypto.com could be a giant Ponzi scheme. After all their crypto credit service offers some of the highest interest rates in crypto. Well what I will say is this crypto.com have been working on building their ecosystem for years. They acquired the crypto.com domain for over ten million dollars and have partnerships with the likes of Visa and Ledger. Let's also not forget that your fiat bounces are covered by FDIC insurance. So I think it's highly unlikely that crypto.com is some form of ponzi scheme. All that being said there are a few things I don't like about the app. The major one is that the crypto.com wallet is completely centralized. That means you do not hold your private keys and you're trusting crypto.com with your funds. There are rumblings that the team are trying to decentralize all that, but as things stand it's a centralized wallet so just be aware of that. I also really dislike the Fiat withdrawal fee to withdraw to an external wallet.

Crypto.com is upfront about that but I don't like that one bit. When it comes to crypto tracking I need to level with you; there are far better options out there like Delta or Blockfolio which I have discussed in my other book called Bitcoin and Cryptocurrency Trading for Beginners with the subtitle of must have tools, Best Exchanges and Trading Strategies. Another thing that is deliberately obvious is that crypto.com is using this app to drive the demand of their MCO and CRO tokens. Basically to unlock any worthwhile features you'll need to get your hands on some. I understand that token utility is super important however it would be nice to be able to get a crypto.com card using Bitcoin or some other crypto. All things being said, there are a host of features and top-notch functionality in this app and I'm sure many of you will absolutely love it. I have to hand it to the Devs at crypto.com the interfaces are super slick and straightforward to use.

Assume you want to pick an altcoin gem. That next low-cap cryptocurrency they've got 10, 20 or even a hundred times and take your crypto portfolio to the moon. I know many people who banked a stack full of cash from investing in undervalued and hidden altcoins. However in today's idiosyncratic markets that has become a lot easier said, than done. So then how do you find those hidden diamonds in the crypto market? Well, in the following chapters I will explain exactly what you need to know to do that. I'll take you through some methods that have been used by various people and made them rich. There are a lot of altcoins out there. Too many to count. Most of them are sh*tcoins But those golden nuggets do exist. You need to start the process of finding those golden nuggets with a top-down approach. An extremely simple initial screening mechanism to get a shortlist of coins that you want to drill deeper into. Perhaps the simplest of all these is market cap. This is because it's easily available for all kinds and there are a number of tools that track this info quite effectively. It's also essential for your selection of the coins you want to target as you can immediately eliminate those that you know not likely to really ten times or so in the near future. You need to find those coins that have really small market caps and hence have the most opportunity to really grow like that. For example if you take a look at all those coins in the top 100 of market cap over at CMC, it's pretty unlikely that these will increase as much as a coin that is sitting at around 300 in market cap. Why is this? Well it's just simple maths. You're already starting at such a high base. It's a lot harder to take a project with a market cap of 50 million to 500 million, than it is to take another coin with a market cap of 2 million to 20 million. So will then have to set out an acceptable range that we think our altcoin gem could be in, and then eliminate all those that are not candidates. There are a number of market cap tracking tools out there including Coinmarketcap, CoinGecko or CoinCodex. For this screening process I usually use Coinmarketcap. This is just because they have a pretty neat filter where you can select the market cap range. You can also drill down further with other metrics something which I will explain in a bit. Generally I like to look at those that are below 10 million dollars in market cap. This should give the coin enough Headroom to really multiply in price should its real value be realized in the market. I usually have a lower bound of about 5 million dollar market cap as well. It's not a hard stop, as there may be a few interesting projects below this cutoff. However the bulk of coins below this market cap are sh*tcoins. They have very little adoption and awareness and even if they have great tech, they're being crowded out.

So now I have my list of coins that I can start focusing in on. This then calls for another filter to further clear the field. The next metric that I'll look at is the volume. This is an important metric as it shows just how active the trading of the coin is. It can also be a great way if you to spot coins that have artificial or abnormal value. Those that may have some wash trading going on. So I like to look at those coins that take about two to six days to turn over their market cap. Put another way, the 24-hour volume should be between 10 to 50% of the market cap. You can't filter a ratio of two metrics on CMC, but you can easily just copy the data over to a spreadsheet and run your own custom filter over it. You can develop a simple Google sheet where you can manually copy the data into. There are ways to develop dynamic screening tools on CMC that use the API but these don't work too well for the lower market cap altcoins. Once you have the ratio of the coins volume to its market cap, you can also run an Excel filter over this so that you are only looking at those coins that you want. Those with a ratio of between 10 to 50%. After applying this filter I have the about 50 altcoins which I will further have to investigate. I need to make absolutely sure that the volume is completely legitimate and not compromised of any wash trading. We've already screened out the most of the coins at wash trading by zoning in on the volume. However to make doubly sure we also have to look at their exchange listings. Indeed seeing where a coin is listed is another important metric as you are after all going to be buying it there. You want to know that you can easily get your hands on and liquidate when you see fit. Here, if a coin only trades on one exchange with a dodgy track record then you should avoid it. Moreover if a coin is to really rally in price, it has to be on an exchange that has a large user base. An exchange where more people get exposed to it are aware of it and can consequently buy it. For browsing through the best exchanges I prefer to use CoinGecko as I find their rankings to be a bit more independent. So now you should take one of the coins you currently have in your refined list and take a look at the exchanges where it's listed. Next, hop on over to CoinGecko and search for the coin. You can select markets and this will show you a list of all the exchanges where the coin is trading. You can see that CoinGecko assigns a trust score to these exchanges. If you see that the coin you picked volume is currently taking place on an exchange you might have never heard of and they are not your top pick that might be already a red flag. However you can also just take a look at that market depth. Market depth is another way to think about liquidity. Those coins that have deeper order books have more liquidity and hence are easier to trade with larger block orders. However if you see that it is listed on Binance that could be potentially good. Most can agree that Binance is a pretty reputable exchange with deep liquidity and reasonable volume. It also has the highest web traffic among the exchanges and the most users. So this is a great sign for the future potential trading of the token. Those are most of the market metrics that I use to zoom in on the coins that are worth doing a bit of deeper digging.

Once you have this list, you can take a look at some important network metrics. Onchain metrics are important. They show whether a cryptocurrency is being used. Whether it's active and not just a nice concept. There are a number of metrics that you can look at here from address activity to network participation on staking coins to total transactions. In fact there are so many metrics to look at that it could be hard to have positive signs from all of them. One cannot really use the same network valuation metrics for all coins like this than they do for large cap old coins. There are a number of tools that you can use to see these stats but one of the best out there has to be IntoTheBlock. Their website is at https://www.intotheblock.com/

They have a overabundance of data and it's not just resigned to network metrics. They offer a 7-day free demo but the paid packages are not that bad at all for what you get. The first metric you should be looking at is the percentage of active addresses compared to total addresses. This can give you an idea of how many people are really using the network compared to how many are just sitting with their tokens in the wallets. Activity in this case is of course transactions to and from said address. As you can know that tell those are the very low ratio are less desirable. Of course you could have a situation where both addresses and transactions are increasing at the same rate in which case the ratio will be constant. So you can also take a look at both of these ratios independently. If both are growing, that is a good sign. Another neat stat that IntoTheBlock has is the time between transactions. This is another stat that you can use to give you an idea of just how active this blockchain is. Moving away from unchanged stats you will also want to possibly examine the distribution of tokens on the network. Centralization is generally not something that you want in a project as it means that Wales can control the market.

Now that we have been through some of the most important on chain metrics that help you determine how active the network is but what about a development activity. This is why I like to dive into the github repos of a project. It's perhaps one of the most transparent ways for me to ascertain development activity. One of the only ways that an altcoin can separate itself from the crowd is with impressive tech and this needs to be worked on constantly. It's not really about being able to read the code that underpins the protocol. You just want to see a regular stream of commits in the core repositories. You want to make sure that there is active discussion in these repositories. If they link to their github then you can go over to the insights section and you'll see the commits, code frequency and contributors. If your token is active with a regular stream of commits and additions or deletions that's great. You can then head on over to the issues tab and see the discussion around the code additions. I should caution you that sometimes you don't get the full picture of development on the public code repositories. Not all commits are created equal and often developers or code in private repositories before they push it live. If you think this could be the case then you could head on over to their development Docs or blog to see what they say about it. Now we've been through the screening process without even looking at any of the projects. This is why important to have a top-down screening process in order to zoom in on those projects that could be interesting. The next stages of the analysis actually involve doing due diligence on the projects themselves and that takes a lot more time. Now that we have our list of projects that we want to research we can finally look into some other specific information. If you know many investors in the venture capital realm, you'll hear that on many occasions they mostly back the team. If the startup has a great team then that's already a major hurdle cleared for the startup business plan itself. As such, you should also place a large emphasis on this when initially doing your research. A team comprised of individuals who have a background in the space is really important. You should also make 100% certain that all of their information is publicly available and verifiable. I remember back in the 2017 ICO craze when fake team credentials were used to promote a project. It's important to verify credentials. Check out their LinkedIn, github, Twitter and other social 's. When doing so it's also important to make sure that their skills and background are aligned. I generally prefer it when a project has a developer heavy team. This is after all is all about cutting edge technology so this should be a preference. It does also help to have people on board who have a business or marketing background as they can help forge partnerships, which could increase adoption and awareness. However unusually a bit turned off when most of the team members are marketers and self-aggrandizing shills. We have enough of that in crypto. There are still a few projects including a pretty well-known one that have pseudonymous developers. Satoshi did create the most valuable blockchain in the world but in today's day and age it helps to know who is behind a project. There is a sea of ICOs that manage to exit scam because no one knew who they were.

Once you've done your research and are pretty happy with the team behind the project, it's time to look at the white paper. I know that many people try to avoid reading over the white paper but this is a shame. There is so much important information that you can glean from doing so. Moreover, a really fluffy white paper could be another sign that you should avoid it. You should also read it with a pinch of salt as it may not be fully updated. However it's an important first step in order to get a vague understanding of what the project is about. You don't have to study it inside and out, just have to focus on some of the most important points and whether they make sense. Some of these include; consensus method, technology stack, interoperability, scalability, use cases and roadmap. Let's take a look at each of those individually. The consensus method is important as this helps us determine not only how secure the blockchain is but also whether it's scalable. There are a plethora of consensus protocols out there with our own pros and cons. Some are pretty unique and ingenious. Others are more plain vanilla. It's an important factor you should consider. The technology stack is a pretty broad term but it means the general structure of the network. How broad is it? Are there numerous different layers where additional technology and functionality can be built? How does this technology stack make the project unique amongst all of its peers? Interoperability means a protocol can interact with other block chains and networks. This could help the network access liquidity and applications from other ecosystems. While the project may not be completely interoperable to start, it's great to see a plan to reach that holy grail of connectedness. Scalability is mentioned quite frequently, but simply if a network cannot scale then it will eventually suffer bottlenecks. This is something that we see with some of the most popular blockchains today. If a project has a consensus method that is scalable, then that is a plus. But will they also develop other scaling solutions? Perhaps off chain etc. Use-cases is pretty self-explanatory. The only way that you're really going to get adoption for a network and the currency is whether there are defined and reasonable use cases. You also have to ask yourself whether these use cases make sense or are just a bunch of gibberish. For example who needs a cryptocurrency for dentists? Well, there is a coin that exists for dentist, yet no dentist using it. Finally, we have that roadmap. This may not always be up-to-date in the white paper so I do encourage you to take look on their website if they have it. But basically a road map is an essential part of a growing project. It's one thing to have a theoretical construct of what you want your network to look like, but it's another thing entirely to execute on it. Are there defined goals and timelines in the road map? Is it detailed enough to be able to measure their performance in meeting these goals and timelines? Based on previous milestones, have they met them or constantly pushed it back with delay after delay? While we're on the point of delays I understand that it's sometimes hard to keep to a defined timeline when developing such a promising tech. But there has to come a point where a project has to be adequately penalized for missing these guidelines. There are some projects today that despite having completed ICOs back in 2017 have still not released a main net. As mentioned a lot of this stuff may not be available in the white paper and it may be dated. That is why you should then take a look at what has been going on with the project since it's been released. Apart from the activity in the github, you can also take a look at their blogs, social media and other communication channels to see where the project is going.

Something else that can really help increase the
awareness and adoption of a cryptocurrency is of
course the community. How big is it and how active
are the members. There are a number of simple
tools that you can use to ascertain the size of the
following. If you head on over to CoinGecko you can
get a sense of just how many followers there are
and how active these users are. You can also head
on over back to Chainlink's website and dive deeper
into their social stats. There is an entire section for
that there. Of course for smaller communities and
projects the data can be thin. That's why I like to
dive a little deeper in order to determine exactly
what type of community this is. The dedication of a
project community speaks volumes about the
broader potential. When you jump into the
telegram groups or read through the forums you
can easily get a sense of what type of community
you are dealing with. Is there a lot of thoughtful
discussion going on? Are the users genuinely
interested in the technology and adoption of the
network? Are they helpful and welcoming to new
members? Do they help answer some of their
questions? These are all strong community signals.
If however you see a flood of memes and personal
attacks, it raises a few red flags. People who throw

around the word FUD for a lack of a solid argument, just turn me off of a project. Why is this important? Well a community that is passionate about the project has staying power. They're interested in seeing the cryptocurrency adopted and know the exact reasons as to why it will be. They're also willing to spend the time to make sure that others are aware of the project. It's also known as free marketing. In summary, there are my main criteria that I use when screening for altcoins. There are other factors that I take into account too but I do hope that you are able to use some of these methods to screen for your altcoins. Remember, time is money and if you're able to zoom in on those projects with the most promise really quickly you're already on the right track.

We are all in search of that hidden edge on the markets. That slice of information that when used appropriately can give us outsized gains over the rest of the crowd. The only problem is that most of this information is reserved for a chosen few. Either that or it's ridiculously expensive to attain. But what if I told you there was a cheap and effective way to get hold of this. A free resource to better read the Bitcoin markets and be two steps ahead. Well, in the following chapters I'm going to explain how you can use the Bitcoin options market to your advantage. Not only when it comes to option analysis but also when trying to determine Bitcoin's price direction. All that is to help equip you with the tools you need to get the market edge. I want to start with a quick beginner's overview of options. An option is a financial instrument that gives the holder the right to buy or sell an asset at a pre-specified time and at a pre-specified price. A call option gives you the right to buy the asset, whereas a put option gives you the right to sell the asset. Because these options are instruments that give you optionality there is a cost that comes with them. This is the option premium and it is the price of the option. Options are themselves derivative instruments that are traded on their own market which is separate from the spot market. You can think of it as analogous to the futures and spot markets. There are a lot of variables that will impact on the premium of an option. These are collectively called the "Greeks" and they are inputs into the legendary black skulls pricing equation. If this appears daunting to you don't worry. All you need to understand are the main drivers of an options price. The first thing that i want to introduce you to is the moneyness of the option. This refers to whether an option is in the money or out of the money. Basically, if you're looking at a call option if the spot price "S" is above the strike price "K", then the option is in the money.

Example: $S > K$ options is in the money or ITM.

Conversely, if the spot is below the strike it is out of the money. Example of that is: $S < K$ Options is out of the money or OTM.

When you have the strike equal to the spot then it is at the money. An example of that is: $S = K$ options is at the money or ATM.

For a put option you just flip the arguments for the in or out of the money levels. The moneyness of an option is important as it impacts on the delta variable in the black skulls. Delta is a measure of how sensitive the price of the option is to a change in the price of the underlying asset. Then you have other factors such as the implied volatility. This is also a very important input in an option price and generally the higher the implied volatility, the higher the price of the option. It's only logical. A more volatile asset will demand a higher option price to make up for the risk in said asset. Then you have the time to expiry. This is also generally positively correlated with price. As the longer that you have to expire the more time value you have of the option. The sensitivity of the price of the option to the rate of change in time is called "theta". This time value also makes sense when you think about it. The longer you have till the expiry of the option, the longer the time period in which the option could either be in or out of the money. These are just some of the main factors that will impact on the price of an option and they are perhaps the most important for you to understand if you want to trade them.

It's time to explore how to use the option data to infer market trends and sentiment. Firstly I want to discuss the put call ratio. This is a measure of the ratio of the open interest or the volume of the puts, versus the calls. The open interest is a measure of the total amount of notional outstanding on a futures or options position. The volume is of course the total amount of options or futures that have been traded in a certain period. For example if we're talking about the open interest put call ratio, we're measuring the total notional outstanding value of all puts to that of the notional outstanding value of all calls. So what can we read from a put call ratio? Well it's able to give us a rough idea of general sentiment in the market. If there is more open interest outstanding for puts than calls, then that means there are larger bearish bets than bullish bets. Hence, a put call ratio of greater than one is viewed as more bearish than a ratio of less than one and vice versa. You can also view the put call ratio through time to get a feeling for how this broader market sentiment has changed. The ratio is slightly more than one when viewed with the volume metric and less than one when viewed with the open interest. I generally tend to use the open interest metric as this gives a more reliable indicator of outstanding trades than the total value of all the options being traded. So based on a put call ratio of 1.36, it means that the put option open interest is about 36% more than the corresponding call notional outstanding. On balance option market participants have more puts outstanding than they do calls. You may be wondering why is this relevant? Well, knowing how options traders are positioning themselves can give you a rough idea of which way they expect the spot market to go. And you should not really be fixated on the absolute number of the put call ratio but rather on how it moves. Whether it's increasing or decreasing, this can help give you a better sense of how that sentiment is changing. okay That's the put call ratio. Of course all this gives you is an overview of how the broader market is positioned. It doesn't really allow us to get a direct comparison in the pricing of puts or calls. This is where the option skew comes in.

Option skew is a measure of the relative richness of the put, versus the call options expressed in terms of implied volatility. It's a measure of how much higher the implied volatility of put options with a specific delta are to call options with the same delta. All normalized by the at the money volatility. Here is the equation that's used to calculate the option 25 delta skew.

$$skew_T^{25d} = \frac{\sigma_{Put}^{25d}(T) - \sigma_{Call}^{25d}(T)}{\sigma^{atm}(T)}.$$

As you can see we're trying to get a measure of how much more implied volatility there is on the puts than the calls, relative to a standard measure of the implied volatility. Given the direct relationship between implied volatility and option premiums, you can also view this ratio as a rough measure of how much more the cost of puts are to calls. If we have two options with a similar sensitivity to the price of the underlying asset, how much more are people willing to pay to take on the puts; bearish versus to take on the bullish view with calls. Let's take a look at a quick example. Let's say that the 25 delta options skew is sitting at about 20%. This basically means that the implied volatility of a put option is about 20% greater than that of a call. We can also therefore infer that the price of similar put options is greater than the calls to a similar degree. This therefore means that option buyers are willing to pay more to buy put options, than they are to pay for calls with exactly the same parameters. You can view it as a more bearish sign. We can also say the opposite if the ratio is negative. Much like the case with the put call ratio, you can view the options skew over time. This is helpful as it allows you to get a sense of how the relative value and hence sentiment has changed recently. For example here you can see the 25 delta option skuw on skew.com for the past three months.

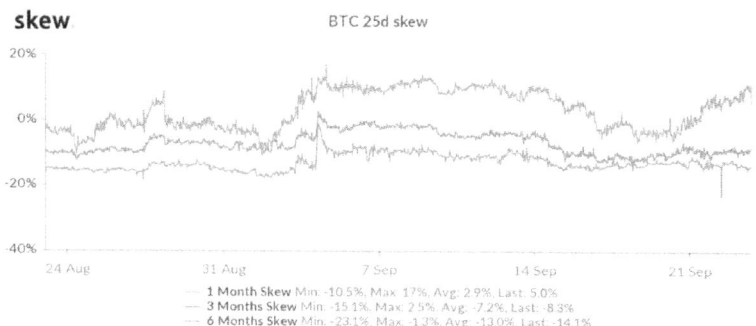

This is for a range of different option expiry times from one month all the way out to six months. If you only look at the three month option skew, you can see this is currently at negative 8.3%. This implies that the call options have a much higher implied volatility and hence the premium is greater than the puts. Generally a bullish sign. However if we take a look at how this has moved over the past three months you can see that it's been trending lower. What we can read from this is that market participants are paying more for calls than the puts. Not only that but the difference has increased over time which shows that their bullishness has too. If you take a look at the spot price of Bitcoin over the period you can see that it's quite well correlated with this fall in the skew. I should also point out that option skew is much broader than just this. You can compare the skew across the entire volatility term structure. You have something called the volatility smile which illustrates this well.

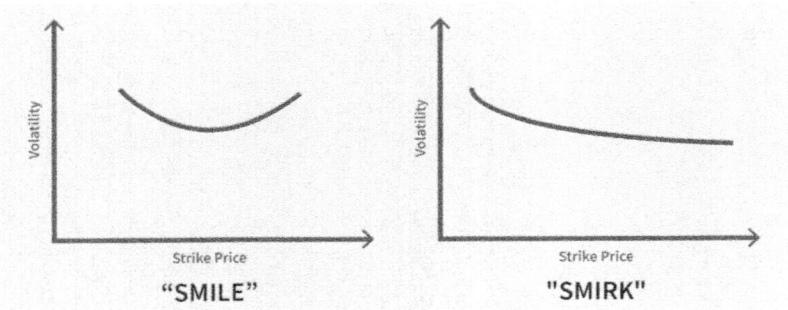

But that's an entirely different topic. All you need to know about option skew is that it's a helpful metric that I often use in order to gauge relative value and sentiment of an option. That's the skew. Now let's take a look at another metric.

It would be great if you could use the option price to calculate the probability of Bitcoin being above a certain price at maturity. Well, that's actually a reality thanks to the black skulls model. Assuming that you have the price of an option as well as all the other parameters in this equation, you can back out the potential price distribution of an asset on expiry. For those of you who did stats at University, you'll know all about probability density functions like the normal distribution.

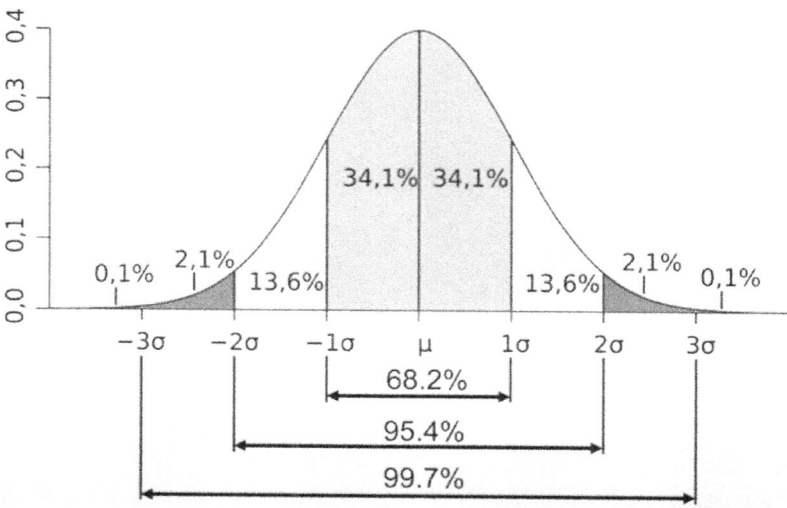

If it's foreign to you, don't worry. All that we're doing here is using the market parameters of the options in order to back out the probability of it being above a chosen strike price. This is also something that you don't have to calculate yourself. skew.com has a graph that calculates this for us. Here you can see the probability distribution for a number of different option expiries. Let's take a look at the December 2020 option just to isolate it.

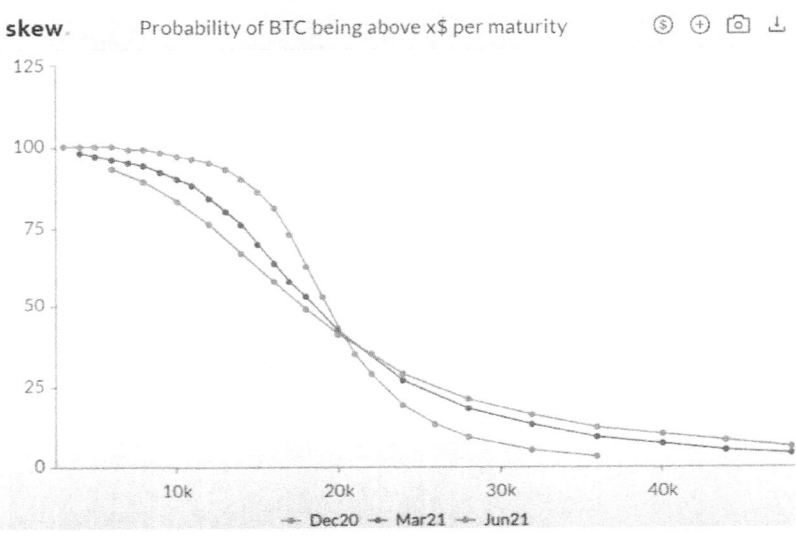

As you can see the probability of the price being above 22k on the 25th of December is about 28%. If we move down more we can see that the probability of being above 24k is about 19%. We can also take a look at the longer term options like the March and June 2021 ones to draw similar probabilities. So what can these probabilities tell you? Well, they can give you a rough idea of how likely certain future prices are based on pricing in the options market. I like to use these as they help to give me a sense of more realistic outcomes. In crypto we're quite desensitized to these parabolic price predictions, so much so that we can sometimes get caught up in the hype. However over on the options market, most of the participants taking out the largest positions are professional investors. I'm talking institutional funds and sophisticated market makers. The prices that they are willing to pay for option protection and exposure are likely to be a better benchmark for their real price predictions than what they claim on TV. Of course I should also caveat that you should not use this as any sort of bible. It's just a probability measure backed out from market data. It's a useful data point you can use in order to further inform your analysis. That is option price probabilities.

Something else that I really want to touch on now is the option expiry dates, more specifically the impact that this tends to have on the spot market. If you follow any sort of crypto news website or trading group, you'll sometimes hear reference to the "option expiry dates". If there are a lot of options that are expiring on the date then this could be an indication that there's likely to be quite a lot of volatility on the day. So the important question here is; why and how can you judge the likely price direction on the expiry date? Let's start with that first one. There is volatility around these expiry dates because market participants are trying to adjust their positions for physical delivery of the underlying asset. Similarly, some market makers may need to adjust their hedge positions in the spot market, as they approach these pivotal moments in the option price. So what you have, is a situation in which option expiry events are having a direct impact on the underlying spot markets. When there's a large number of outstanding options, the impact on the spot market is likely to be that much greater. This is something that's been known in the equity markets for a number of years. These are sometimes termed the expiry weeks where volatility in the underlying share starts to pick up. However given the growth of Bitcoin options, we've also seen these instruments impacting the Bitcoin spot price. This usually tends to happen about two days before the actual expiry. Those participants that hold the option may either close out of their position or roll forward into new options on the expiry date. So we know that options expiry dates are usually dates of interest when it comes to price movements. But, is there a way to get a sense of which way it's likely to move? Well, there's no hard and fast way but you can get a vague idea by taking a deeper look into the options order books themselves. In this case, I'm going to be taking a look at the Deribit order books. They are the exchange with the most liquidity and functionality for retail traders. To logon to Deribit , please visit their website at https://www.deribit.com/

So let's take a look at some options that are about to expire soon. What we're looking for is to determine how much theoretical buying or selling pressure is likely to come in the spot market from the expiry from these calls or puts in the options market. Basically to get a rough back of the envelope put call ratio. Next, you can further the range of options to those that are relatively close to the money level. Here you might choose an acceptable range for both. In my case I'm of the view that on the 21th of December Bitcoin is likely to be within the 21K to 23.5K level. Hence I take a look at all the options that fall into this range. Now I want to try and determine the total outstanding notional or open interest on the call and then the put side. With these option expirations, the total open interest on the calls is about 4200 Bitcoin. Whereas on the put side the total notional outstanding is about 1770 Bitcoin. So, what this shows us is that as we roll forward towards the December 21st expiry date, there are a lot more cool positions in the market; almost 2.4 times more. So theoretically, this means that there is more chance of there being buying pressure in the spot market as we head into the expiry than selling pressure. A more bullishly positioned market. Of course I should caveat that at the time of doing this analysis there was still about two weeks to expiry. A lot can change closer to the expiry date and as I mentioned before in the Bitcoin markets the impact on spot markets of the open expiry only tends to be felt two or three days before. So, if you're going to be using this analysis method, I would encourage you to re-examine the relative open interest balance as we get closer to expiry time. You should also note that this is not a science. There are many other factors that can swing the price on expiry. Let's not forget that you also have the impact of the futures markets as well as large whale orders going through on the spot market. But, it is a handy guide that I use from time to time. The truth is that the particulars of this relationship between the derivatives and spot markets are fascinated. There may be some things here that are hard to grasp and that's totally okay. The truth is that most people who trade options don't really focus too much on the underlying equations. They're more concerned about overarching concepts. Knowing exactly how the 25 delta skew is calculated is of way lesser importance than understanding what it means. What does it show about how the market is positioned and how you can use that information in your broader research toolbox. Similarly, having a rough idea of what price distributions are in the future, can help you adjust your expectations. You can get a rough idea of price probabilities from the options markets and it always helps to keep an eye on option expiry dates. Even if you don't try to conclude a particular price direction, it has been shown these dates cause spot market volatility. By having these dates pinned in your calendar, you're better prepared to deal with any potential volatility that could result. There's nothing worse than being caught off guard by a large price gap; be it up or down. So I hope that you can find some of these indicators and tools helpful in your price analysis. They can be that much more interesting when actually used to trade options themselves.

In this chapter you will learn about candlestick patterns. What is a candlestick? Well, a candlestick is a way of displaying information about an assets price movement. Candlestick charts are one of the most popular components of technical analysis, enabling traders to interpret price information quickly and from just a few price bars. This chapter will focus on a daily chart where in each candlestick details a single day's trading. It has three basic features. The body which represents the open to close range. The wick or shadow that indicates the intraday high and low. The color, which reveals the direction of market movement. A green or white body indicates a price increase, while a red or black body shows a price decrease. Over time individual candlesticks form patterns that traders can use to recognize major support and resistance levels. There are a great many candlestick patterns that indicate an opportunity within a market. Some provide insight into the balance between buying and selling pressures, while others identify continuation patterns or market and decision. Before you start trading, it's important to familiarize yourself with the basics of candlestick patterns and how they can inform your decisions. Bullish patterns may form after a market downtrend and signal a reversal of price movement. They are an indicator for traders to consider opening a long position to profit from any upward trajectory.

Hammer

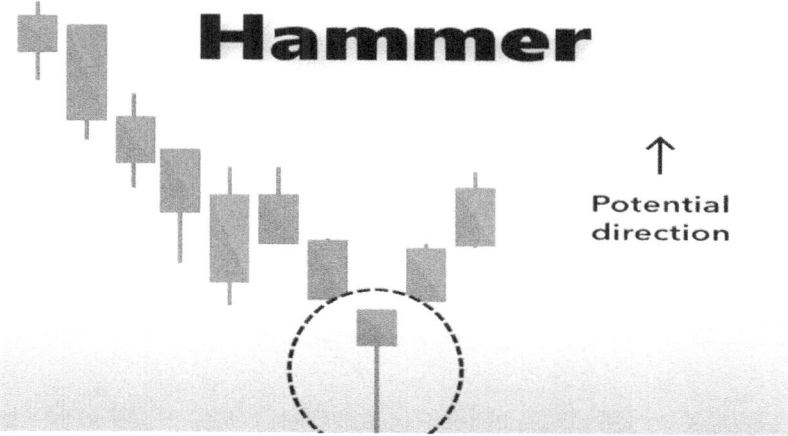

The hammer candlestick pattern is formed of a short body with a long lower wig and is found at the bottom of a downward trend. A hammer shows that although there were selling pressures during the day, ultimately a strong buying pressure drove the price back up. The color of the body can vary, but green hammers indicate a stronger bull market than red hammers.

Inverse hammer

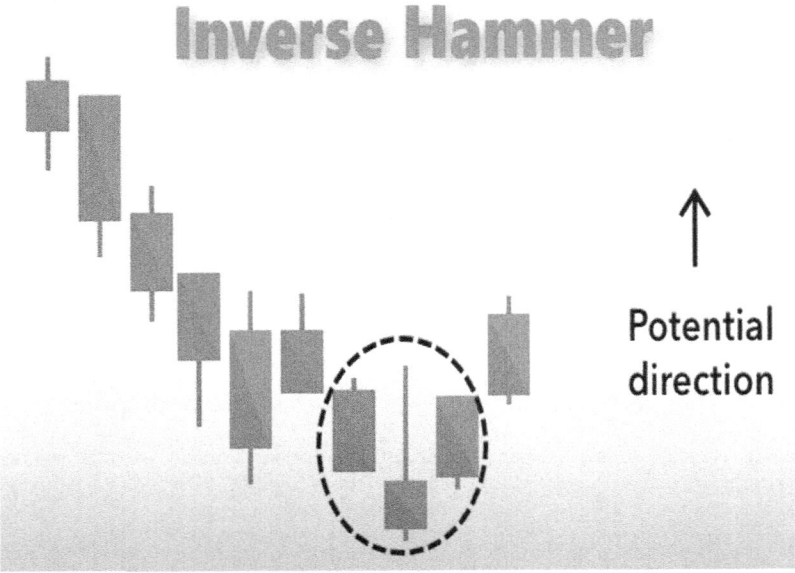

A similarly bullish pattern is the inverted hammer. The only difference being that the upper wick is long, while the lower wick is short. It indicates a buying pressure followed by a selling pressure that was not strong enough to drive the market price down. The inverse hammer suggests that buyers will soon have control of the market.

Bullish engulfing

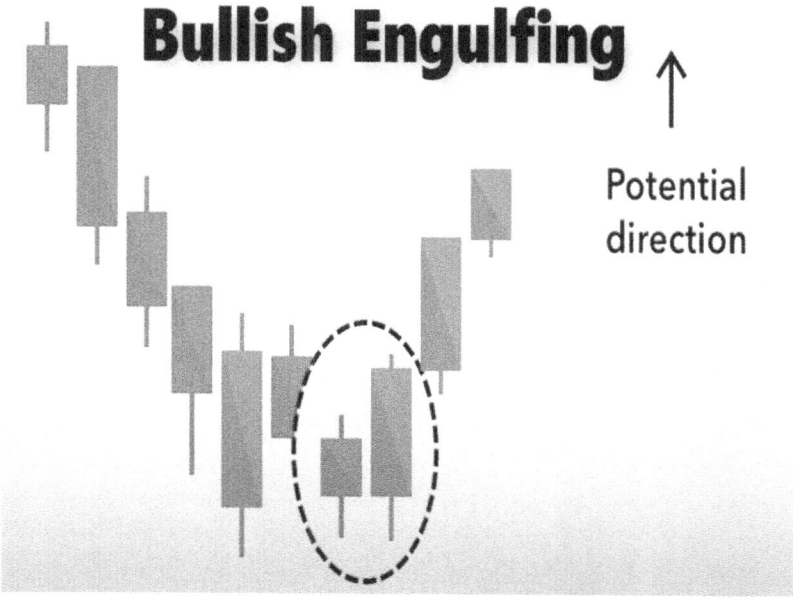

The bullish engulfing pattern is formed of two candlesticks. The first candle is a short red body that is completely engulfed by a larger green candle. Though the second day opens lower than the first, the bullish market pushes the price up. Culminating in an obvious win for buyers.

Piercing line

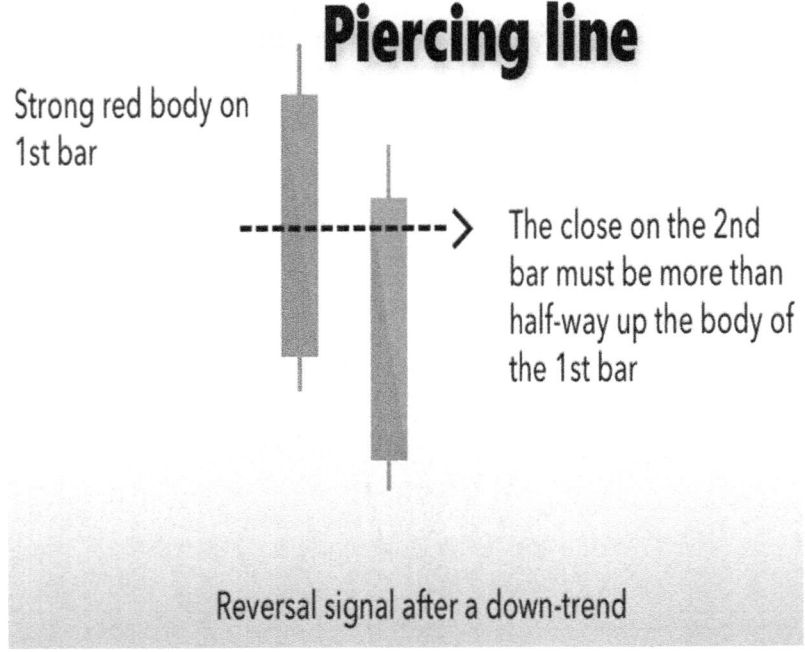

Piercing line

Strong red body on 1st bar

The close on the 2nd bar must be more than half-way up the body of the 1st bar

Reversal signal after a down-trend

The piercing line is also a two stick pattern made up of a long red candle, followed by a long green candle. There is usually a significant gap down between the first candlesticks closing price and the green candlesticks opening. It indicates a strong buying pressure as the price is pushed up to or above the mid price of the previous day.

Morning Star

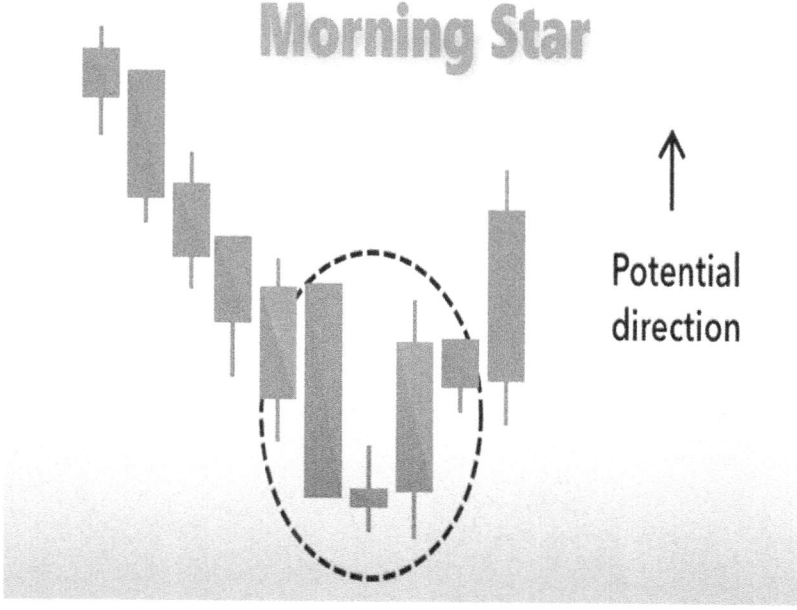

The Morningstar candlestick pattern is considered a sign of hope and a bleak market downtrend. It is a three stick pattern one short bodied candle between a long red and a long green. Traditionally, the star will have no overlap with the longer bodies as the market gaps both on open and closed. It signals that the selling pressure of the first day is subsiding and a bull market is on the horizon.

Three white soldiers

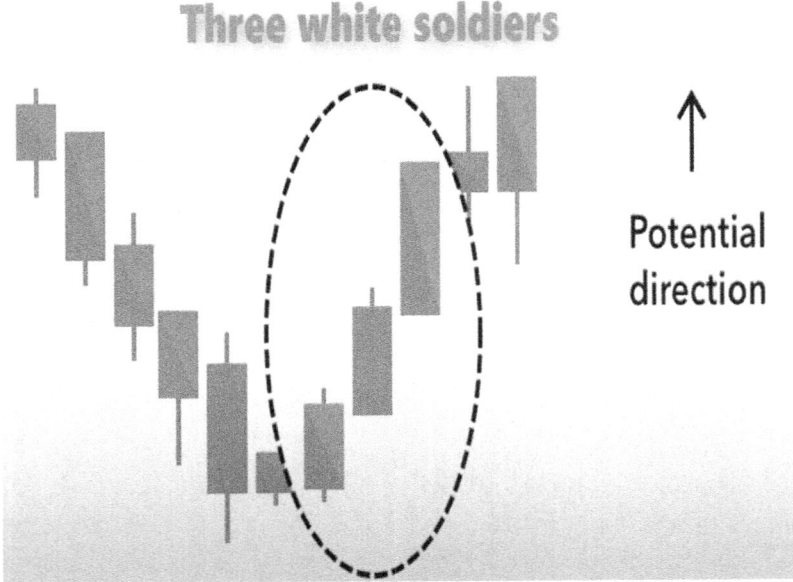

The three white soldiers pattern occurs over three days. It consists of consecutive long green or white candles with small wicks which open and close progressively higher than the previous day. It is a very strong bullish signal that occurs after a downtrend and shows a steady advance of buying pressure.

Bearish candlestick patterns bearish candlestick patterns usually form after an uptrend and signal a point of resistance. Heavy pessimism about the market price often causes traders to close their long positions and open a short position to take advantage of the falling price.

Hanging man

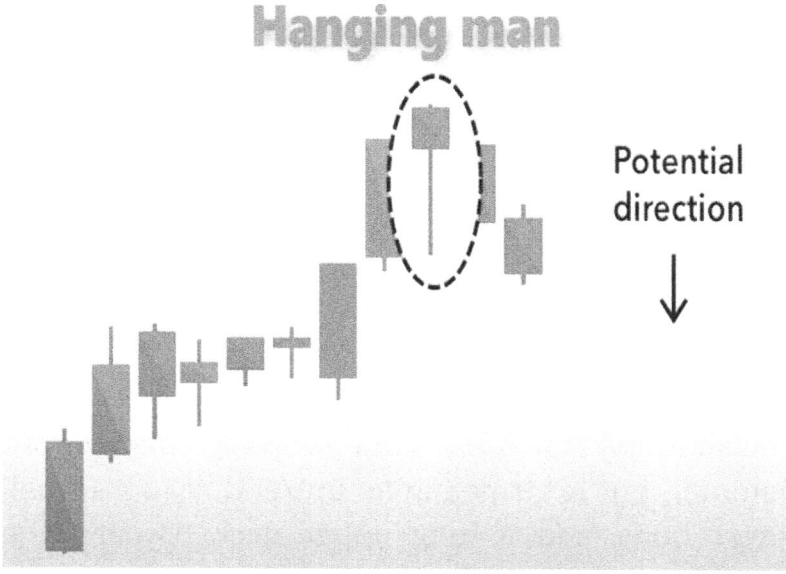

The hanging man is the bearish equivalent of a hammer. It has the same shape but forms at the end of an uptrend. It indicates that there was a significant sell-off during the day, but that buyers were able to push the price up again. The large sell-off is often seen as an indication that the Bulls are losing control of the market.

Shooting star

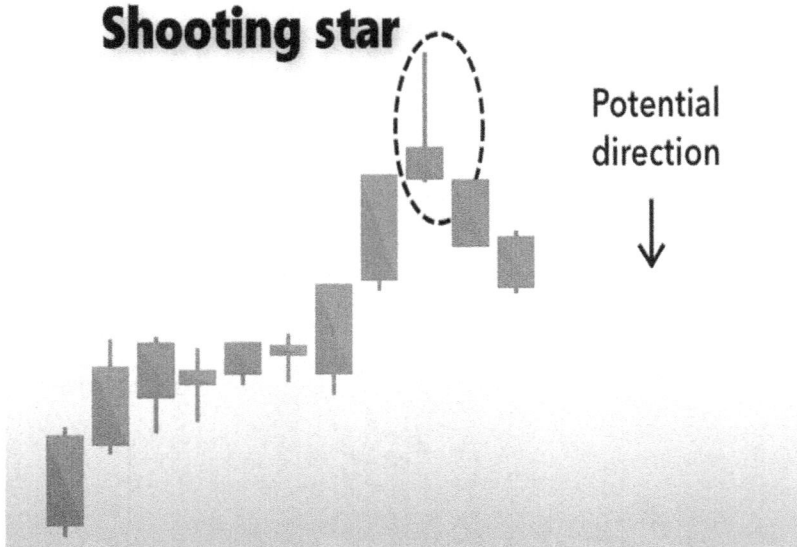

The shooting star is the same shape as the inverted hammer, but is formed in an uptrend. It has a small lower body and a long upper wick. Usually the market will gap slightly higher on opening and rally to an intraday high before closing at a price just above the open. Like a star falling to the ground.

Bearish engulfing

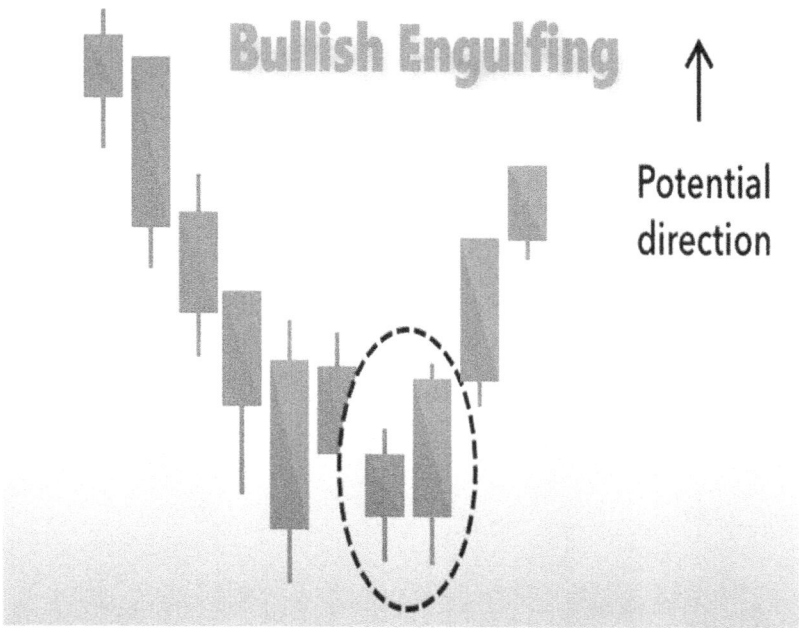

A bearish engulfing pattern occurs at the end of an uptrend. The first candle has a small green body that is engulfed by a subsequent long red candle. It signifies a peak or slowdown of price movement and is a sign of an impending market downturn. The lower the second candle goes the more significant the trend is likely to be.

Evening star

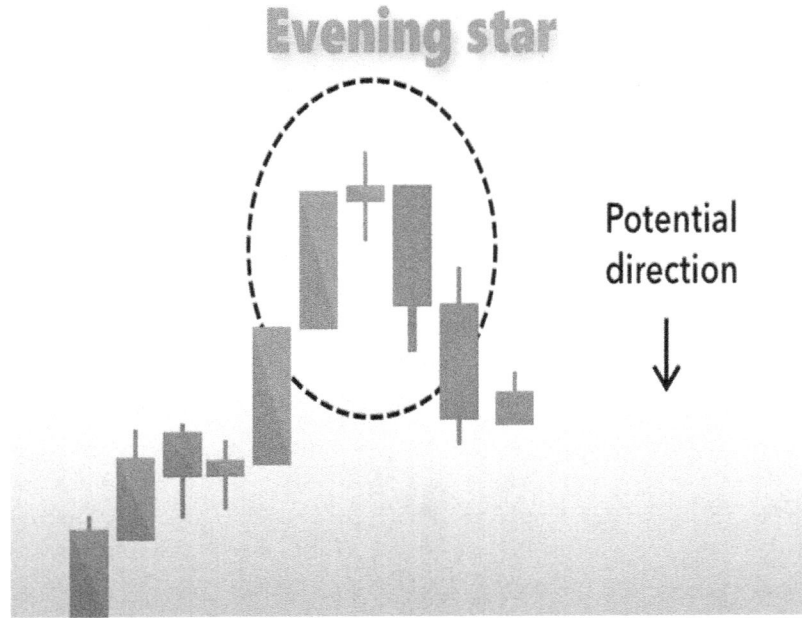

The evening star is a three candlestick pattern that is the equivalent of the bullish Morningstar. It is formed of a short candle sandwiched between a long green candle and a large red candlestick. It indicates the reversal of an uptrend and is particularly strong when the third candlestick erases the gains of the first candle.

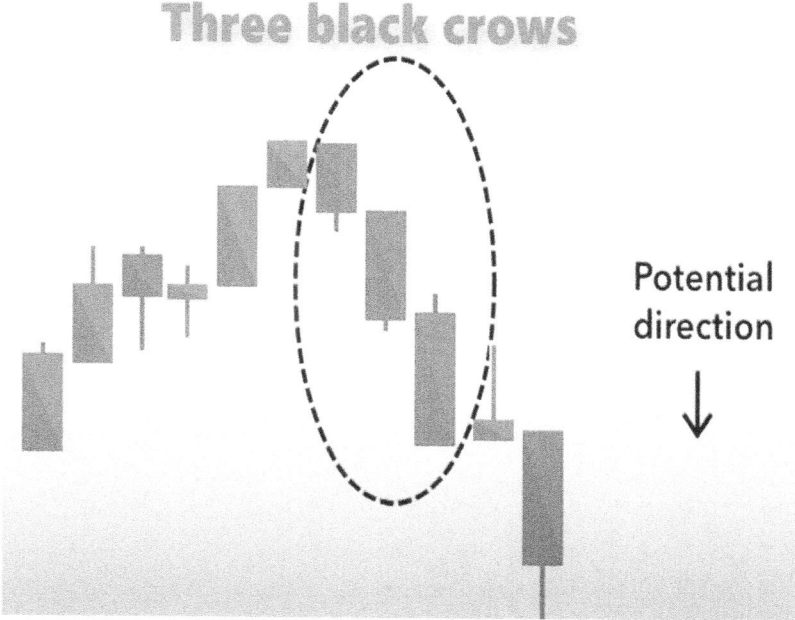

The three black crows candlestick pattern comprises of three consecutive long red candles with short or non-existent wicks. Each session opens at a similar price to the previous day, but selling pressures push the price lower and lower with each close. Traders interpret this pattern as the start of a bearish downtrend as the sellers have overtaken the buyers during three successive trading days.

Dark cloud cover

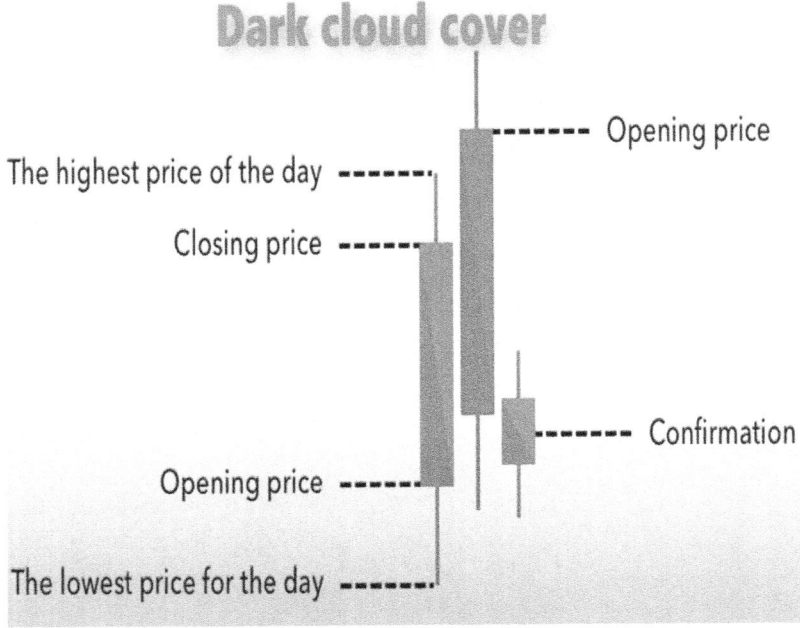

The dark cloud cover candlestick pattern indicates a bearish reversal. A black cloud over the previous day's optimism. It comprises two candlesticks. A red candlestick which opens above the previous green body and closes below its midpoint. It signals that the Bears have taken over the session, pushing the price sharply lower. If the wicks of the candles are short, it suggests that the downtrend was extremely decisive.

For continuation candlestick patterns, if a candlestick pattern doesn't indicate a change in market direction it is what is known as a continuation pattern. These can help traders to identify a period of rest in the market when there is market indecision or neutral price movement.

Doji

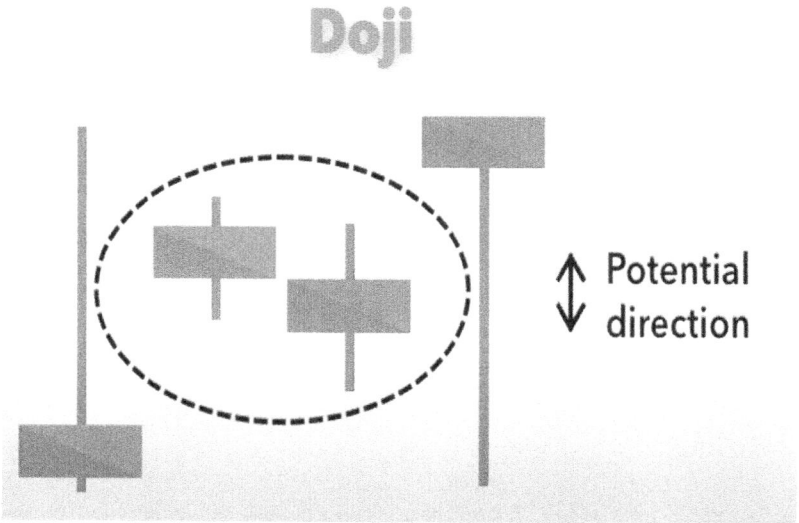

When a markets open and close are almost at the same price point, the candlestick resembles a cross or plus sign. Traders should look out for a short to non-existent body with wicks of varying lengths.

This doji's pattern conveys a struggle between buyers and sellers that results in no net gain for either side. Alone a doji is neutral signal but it can be found in reversal patterns such as the bullish Morningstar in bearish evening star.

Spinning top

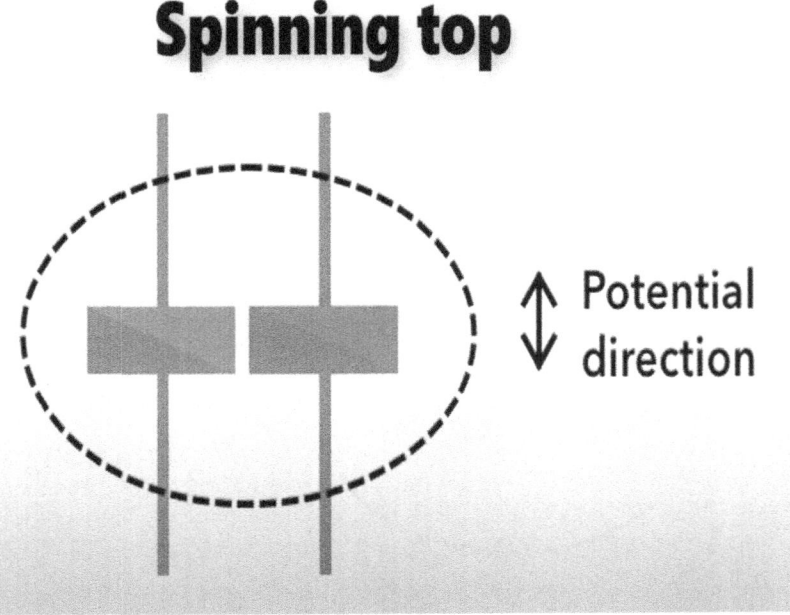

The spinning top candlestick pattern has a short body centered between wicks of equal length. The pattern indicates indecision in the market, resulting in no meaningful change in price. The Bulls sent the price higher while the Bears pushed it low again.

Spinning tops are often interpreted as a period of consolidation, or rest, following a significant uptrend or downtrend. On its own the spinning top is a relatively benign signal, but they can be interpreted as a sign of things to come as it signifies that the current market pressure is losing control.

Falling three methods

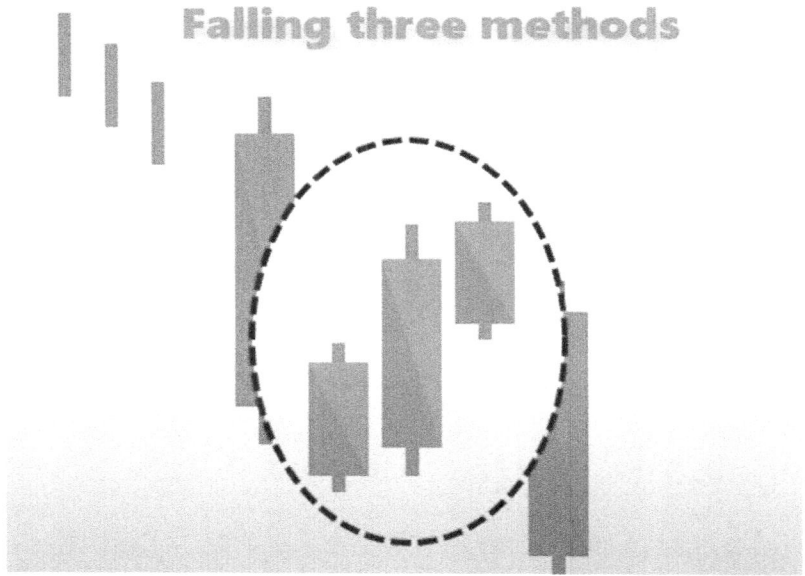

Three methods formation patterns are used to predict the continuation of a current trend; be it bearish or bullish. The bearish pattern is called the falling three methods; it is formed of a long red body followed by three small green bodies and another red body. The green candles are all contained within the range of the bearish bodies. It shows traders that the Bulls do not have enough strength to reverse the trend.

Rising three methods

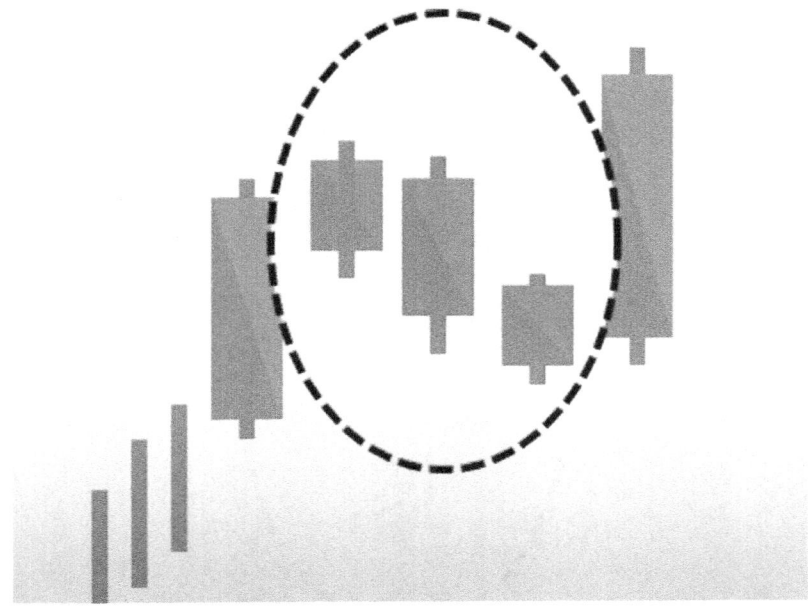

The opposite is true for the bullish pattern called the rising three methods candlestick pattern. It comprises of three short red sandwiched within the range of two long greens. The pattern shows traders that despite some selling pressure, buyers are retaining control of the market.

The best way to learn to read candlestick patterns is to practice entering and exiting trades from the signals they give. If you don't feel ready to trade on live markets, you can develop your skills in a risk-free environment by opening an test account. When using any candlestick pattern, it is important to remember that although they are great for quickly predicting trends, they should be used alongside other forms of technical analysis to confirm the overall trend.

In this chapter I will reveal the secret to trading success and it's probably not what you're expecting. To become a successful trader he needs to know this. Around 90% of all traders lose money, so only 10% manage to be consistently profitable. But what is it that these successful 10% do different than the failing 90%? Well, first let's take a look at the typical trader of the 90% losing traders. Most people that are in this losing category are doing the following. They're somehow hear about trading and they believe that is all about the fancy lifestyle of a successful trader like easy money, work from anywhere in the World, expensive cars and the list goes on. They filled with motivation and greed. These people then sign up to the best broker that they probably found through some misleading commercial. Some people even watch one or two random YouTube trading videos before depositing their money to the broker platform. After signing up they usually start buying random stocks due to random reasons. To their surprise, the stocks rarely shoot up in price more from the not they exit their positions with a loss. Before they know it, they become part of the 90% losing trader group. Clearly not all losing traders go through these stages but a big deal of them do. I'm not saying this to mock the losing traders. I'm simply trying to compare losing to winning traders. My point is that consistently profitable traders actually know what they're doing. They usually have years of experience laid out and test the trading system. Furthermore, profitable traders have a trading plan and before they enter any trade, they know what they will do for changes in their position. In other words trading isn't easy. If it would be easy everyone would be doing it. Let's compare trading to other professions now. Would you try to fly an airplane without any guidance, education and practice? If you would, it would probably end through quite bad. Or would you try to perform a heart surgery without going to med school without any practice experience or education? Chances are high that you answered no to the previous two questions. To become a surgeon or pilot or anything else you normally need to go through years of training studying and practice. Why should this be different for trading? Just like no one is born as a perfect heart surgeon, no one is born as a perfect profitable trader. You need to study, practice and work your way up. If you try to fly an airplane without any education you would probably crash and blow up. The same goes for your trading account. Trading without any education, usually leads to you blowing up your account. Don't make the mistake and risk your hard earned money without educating yourself before. The key takeaway here is that you need education to become a profitable trader. The next question is; do you need paid education or can you learn how to trade for free? Both free and paid trading education have their advantages and disadvantages. First of all let's take a look at the advantages of paid education. One major advantage of paid education is the motivational aspect. People tend to be more committed to things that they actually paid for. This is because they feel like something is on the line. A further advantage is the focus on one strategy. Most good paid trading courses focus on one strategy and teach you everything important for that particular strategy. Most paid education is therefore more specific and relevant than free education. In other words, many paid trading courses of higher quality than free courses. In addition to that, premium costs often come with personal support. Let's move on to the advantages of free education. The most obvious Pro is the fact that it's free. If the free education is bad, it doesn't matter because you didn't pay anything for it. Next up other disadvantages of the paid trading courses. First of all one disadvantage is the fact that it costs money, therefore something is on the line. If the education is poor quality, you wasted your money. Some of these so-called trading courses are scams so be careful. Another major disadvantage is the lack of transparency. Many trading educators earn all the money from their trading education and nothing from that trading. Just because someone tells you he is a massively profitable trader, does not mean that he actually is. The last but not least, the fact that paid education is very specific is also a disadvantage. It is always good to have a wide general knowledge. Most paid courses focus on their strategies and ignore the bigger picture. Lastly, we have the cons of the free education. Often free trading courses can be less thorough therefore it can generally be hard to find very good and in-depth free trading courses. Thus free education requires a little more work. Before we move on I just want to say that these pros and cons are generalizations. Not all of the advantages and disadvantages applied to all free and paid trading courses. Obviously there are exceptions. As you can see both free and paid trading courses have their advantages and disadvantages. It can be quite hard to pick one over the other. In my opinion it's best to combine free and paid trading education. This will let you take advantage of the pros of both free and paid education. I recommend starting with free education. All basic trading concepts can be learned from free education. I do not recommend spending any substantial amount of money just to learn the basics. You should be able to learn very important basic concepts such as asset types, basic charting, risk management and so on from free education. After doing this, I suggest asking some questions.

Are you still interested in trading? Are you still willing to put in more work to learn how to trade? If yes, what trading style fits you? Aspects to consider here are starting capital, time, risk tolerance and so on. As you learned about different asset types, you should have an idea of what asset types fits you. Next, I recommend looking at paid training courses. You should already have a fundamental understanding of trading and the markets in general. Ideally you should also have a preferred asset type like options, stocks, cryptocurrency. When trying to find a good trading course, you should do some research. Try to find a course that fits you, your starting capital, your the time and so on. Look for proven track records and success stories. Generally, if something sounds too good to be true it probably is. Please don't skip the research part. There are countless scams out there so be careful. This is one of multiple ways to learn how to trade but you can do it differently as well. For example you could just pay for everything if you have more than enough money but remember; only the very last step is trading. Don't risk your hard earned money before you actually know what you're doing. Otherwise you will just end up like 90% of all traders. Before starting to trade real money, you should have a good understanding of trading at the markets. You should also have a proven profitable system a concrete trading plan and you should have had loads of education. Even after you start Trading, you should try to continue to learn more. Never follow random trade alerts. Never rely on one or two random indicators. Never listen to seemingly magic trading software. Just do it the right way. Educate yourself and learn how to trade. Remember, if it would be easy everyone would be doing it. The last piece of the puzzle is trading like is your profession and not as a hobby. The secret to trading success is the same as the secret to success in general. It's hard work, experience, education, taking action and practice.

In this chapter you will learn everything you need to know about implied volatility, what implied volatility rank is and why it matters. First of all, what is implied volatility? Well, implied volatility can be derived from options pricing models such as the Black Scholes options pricing model. It can be thought of as they expected likelihood of certain price changes in the underlying asset. But what does that mean? Well, to understand this let's break down what goes into an options price. The black Scholes formula uses the following variables to calculate an options price. The underlying price, the strike price, the expiration date, the risk-free rate and implied volatility. The first two factors are quite obvious because they determine the intrinsic value of an option. The expiration date also makes a lot of sense as more time to expiration gives your position, more time to work. Thus time to expiration should definitely affect the price of an option. The risk-free rate only has a very small effect on an options price and doesn't change significantly over short periods of time therefore it can be ignored for now. Last but not least the volatility of the underlying asset should also affect the options price because more volatile assets tend to give an options trader more opportunity to profit from price swings, whereas on volatile assets have limited trading opportunities. For instance, a far out of the money option is far more likely to become in the money if the underlying asset is very volatile then if it's not. Therefore volatility is one of the factors used to calculate a theoretical options price. However, it's fairly easy to observe and measure the underlying price, strike price and time to expiration. But it's not as straightforward to measure the volatility of the security, especially not the future volatility. That's why models such as the Black Scholes Model use a formula to determine the implied volatility from the options price instead of the options price from the implied volatility. An options price can be observed in the markets together with all the other factors except for volatility. From all this you can calculate a theoretical volatility value. This volatility value is implied from the options price, therefore it's called implied volatility. So when you hear in some financial news that options traders are expecting upcoming volatility, what they're really saying is that the volatility implied by the current option prices, where the implied volatility is relatively high. Note that implied volatility is not the same as historical volatility. Historical volatility is the past actual volatility and it does not affect the options price, whereas implied volatility does. Furthermore, implied volatility is a purely theoretical value therefore implied volatility values often differ from the actual volatility values over certain time periods. Hopefully this helps you understand what implied volatility is.

Well, first of all it's one of the main factors affecting an options price. This alone is one reason why you should pay attention to IV. Furthermore, implied volatility can give you insight into what kind of volatility the market is expecting. You can compare the expected volatility to your own analysis and potentially build a position around the difference in these two. An options trader should always look at implied volatility as well as the underlying trading price, expiration date and strike price before putting on a position. It's also possible to use implied volatility to calculate the expected price range of an underlying asset until the expiration date. To understand this let's first take a look at a normal distribution diagram.

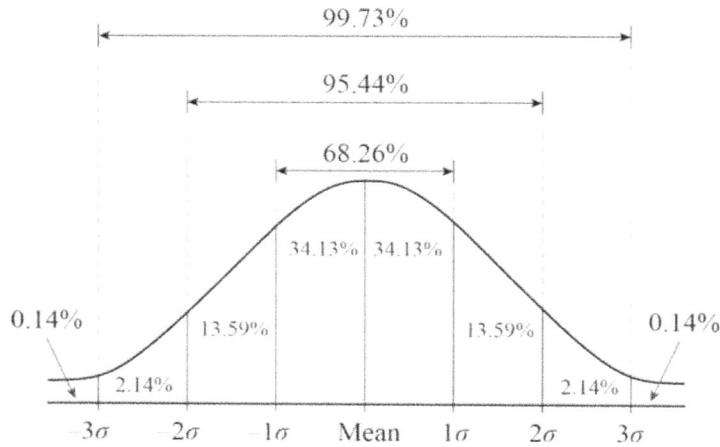

Depending on which model you use, you might assume that stock price changes are distributed like this. That would mean that 68% of the time price only changed slightly and the bigger a price move is, the less likely it becomes. The one standard deviation move for less happens about 68% of the time. The two standard deviation move where anything less happens about 95% of the time and so on. This isn't necessarily a very realistic distribution for prices because bigger moves happen far more often than they should according to a normal distribution. Furthermore, prices can move more to the up side than they can to the downside. Nevertheless, a normal distribution is commonly used and it helps to understand what the expected move of an asset is. If you use the normal distribution you can calculate the expected move of an asset through this formula. One standard deviation equals, plus or minus implied volatility, times the underlying price, times the square root of the time to expiration divided by 365. Two standard deviations can be calculated by multiplying the one standard deviation move by two and so on.

Expected Price Range

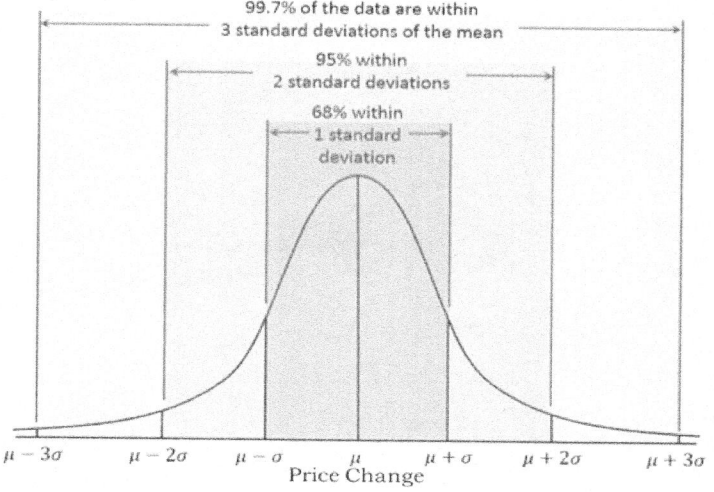

99.7% of the data are within
3 standard deviations of the mean

95% within
2 standard deviations

68% within
1 standard
deviation

$\mu - 3\sigma$ $\mu - 2\sigma$ $\mu - \sigma$ μ $\mu + \sigma$ $\mu + 2\sigma$ $\mu + 3\sigma$

Price Change

Implied volatility is normally quoted on an annualized basis. That's why we divide the time to expiration by 365 to get the expected range until the expiration date. Let's look at an example to clarify all this. Currency XYZ is trading at $100. We will first look at an option with 30 days left till expiration and an implied volatility of 40%. So the one standard deviation range over the next 30 days is plus minus 0.4, times 100, times the square root of 30, divided by 365. This is about plus minus 11.5 which means the one standard deviation range over the next 30 days is 88.5 dollars till 111.5 dollars. This means that the markets expect XYZ's price to stay between about 88 and 112 dollars over the next 30 days with about 68% probability.

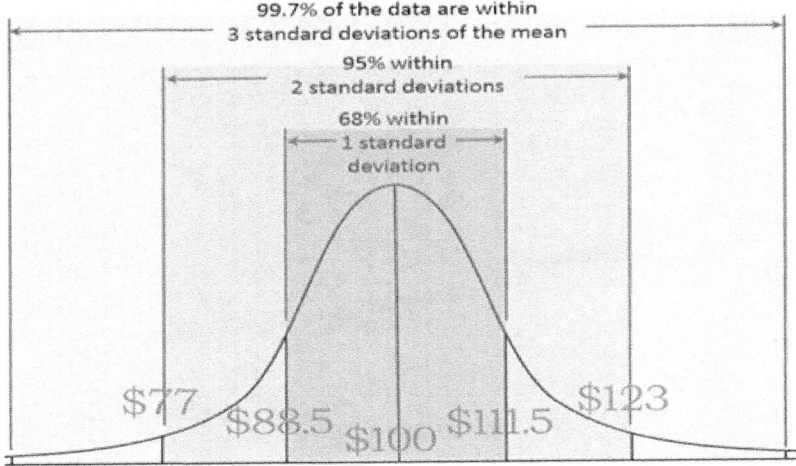

The two standard deviation move would be up to 123 dollars were down to $77. Now let's take a look at the same asset with the same implied volatility but 60 days instead of 30 days to expiration. The one standard deviation range would now be about 84 dollars to $116. The two standard deviation range would be 68 to $132. This makes sense because XYZ can obviously move much more in 60 days than it can in 30 days.

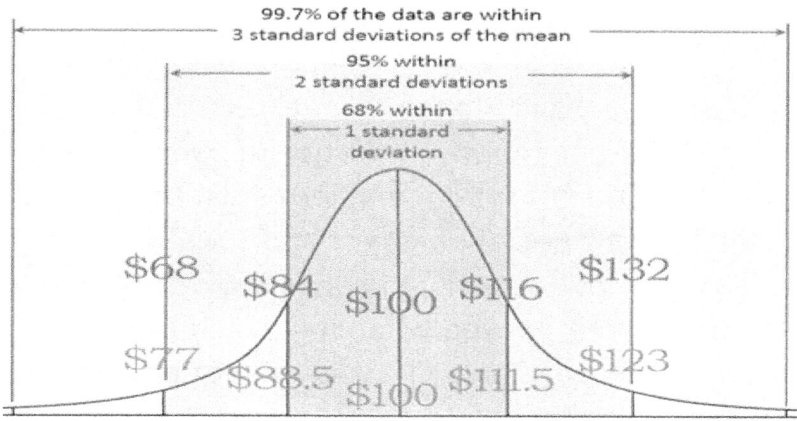

99.7% of the data are within
3 standard deviations of the mean

95% within
2 standard deviations

68% within
1 standard
deviation

$68 $84 $100 $116 $132

$77 $88.5 $100 $111.5 $123

Note that all of this assumes that the distribution of prices is normal. This is not necessarily a very realistic assumption. Therefore in practice other distributions such as the log normal distribution or other ones are used much more commonly. Nevertheless, this simplified explanation of the expected move should give you a good idea of what the expected move is and how you can use it for your trading. Luckily, you will never really have to calculate the expected move yourself as most good broker platforms will calculate it for you.

By now you have hopefully realized that implied volatility is an important factor to look at when trading options. When implied volatility is high options are priced higher and when implied volatility is low options are priced lower. But how do you know if implied volatility is high or low? For instance, if an assert XYZ has an option with an implied volatility of 40% and asset ABC has an option with an implied volatility level of 30%, what does that mean? Well, just because the absolute implied volatility value of XYZ is higher than of ABC, we can't just assume that it's implied volatility is higher relative to itself. Let me give you a more specific example to clarify this. Let's say XYZ is usually a very volatile asset and has an average implied volatility of 70%. But now the IV dropped down to 40%, whereas ABC tends to have an IV level of around 20% most of the time. But now it's implied volatility has gone up to 30% and this means that ABC's implied volatility is relatively high and XYZ is implied volatility, is relatively low even though XYZ's absolute volatility is greater than ABC's. I hope that this explains that it's very hard to compare the implied volatilities of different assets, because different assets can have very different trading characteristics. To solve this problem, we can use implied volatility rank. IV rank looks at the past year of implied volatility data of an assets and then tells you how the current level of IV is relative to the past 365 days. IV rank is always a value between 0 and 100. 100 being the highest and 0 the lowest level of applied volatility over the past year. Here is a brief example. Asset ABC has an IV rank of 20. This means that it's implied volatility is relatively low because it has been much higher throughout the past year. Therefore you can assume that ABC's options are relatively cheap compared to past times. If on the other hand IV rank would be at 100, you know that ABC's implied volatility has never been higher over the past year and therefore this could be a good time to sell options because they are very expensive. In summary, implied volatility rank brings some context to implied volatility. Here is the formula that is most commonly used to calculate IV rank. The current IV level minus the 52-week IV low, divided by the 52-week IV high, minus the 52-week IV low and all of this is multiplied by 100 to get the IV rank.

$$\text{IV Rank} = \frac{(\text{Current IV} - 52\ \text{Week IV Low})}{(52\ \text{Week IV High} - 52\ \text{Week IV Low})} * 100$$

Note that some brokers often filter out very extreme implied volatility values from the past 52 weeks so that IV rank isn't skewed or distorted by these values. Don't worry you won't have to calculate this yourself because once again most good brokers will do this for you. Certain platforms even allows you to scan and filter assets by IV rank. This is one of the easiest ways to find assets with very low or very high implied volatility values. I hope this helps you understand implied volatility and how implied volatility rank works.

While most people like to think that they are rational, most humans aren't very rational. Especially when money is on the line and time is scarce human decision making can be very flawed. Trading is one of the fields where erroneous and irrational behaviour patterns are especially common. In this chapter we're going to look at the most common cognitive biases and irrational decision making patterns and how to avoid them. Being aware of these thinking flaws has two main advantages. Firstly, it helps you avoid them in your own trading and secondly it can help you identify and explain seemingly irrational market behaviors caused by these biases. Most of these so-called cognitive biases were discovered and introduced by the Nobel winning Daniel Kahneman and Amos Tversky. The first cognitive bias that I want to talk about is the gambler's fallacy. The gambler's fallacy is incorrectly over or understating the likelihood of an event based on a series of past events. This can be illustrated with a simple example of a coin flip. The probability that a coin will land on heads is 50%. No matter how often you flip a coin this probability does not change. So even if your coin just landed on heads 10 times in a row, this does not affect the probability of the next coin flip. Like the name implies, the gambler's fallacy is especially common in gambling. But this pattern of thinking is quite common in trading as well. Let me give you some examples. Have you ever opened a long position because a stock had many consecutive down days or vice versa? If so, you have fallen prey to the gambler's fallacy. Another example would be the reaction to a losing or winning streak. If you ever felt that after many consecutive wins the chances of losing increased and you decreased your position size, you have been guilty of the gambler's fallacy. The odds of winning on a trade, don't magically change just because you had multiple losses or wins before this trade. Speaking of winning streaks if we assume that you found a trading strategy that guarantees you a 70% chance of winning on every single trade, what do you think the odds of winning 10 times in a row are? Well, the answer is under 3%. In fact, even the probability that you will have two consecutive wins with this strategy is under 50%. This means it is less likely that you will have two consecutive winners than that you won't. And remember, this is with a strategy that guarantees you 70% chance of success on each trade. Most strategies won't have nearly as good odds. To calculate the probability of "n" consecutive wins you simply have to take the estimated odds of your trading strategy to the power of "n".

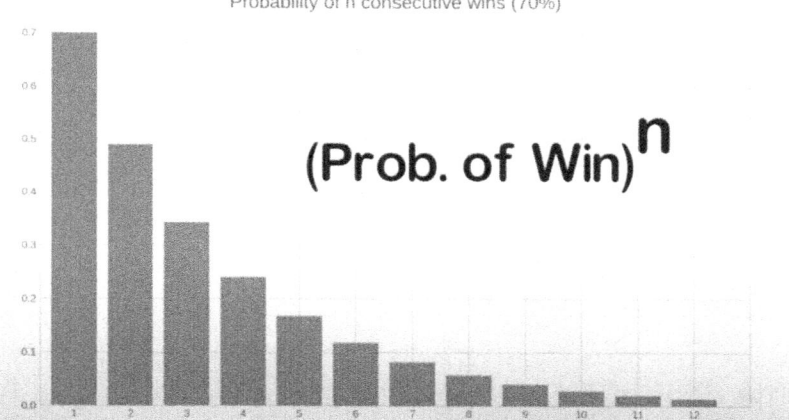

$$(\text{Prob. of Win})^n$$

Note that this assumes that the trades are independent from each other and the probability of winning is constant. If we look at the odds of losing streaks we get a similar picture. Here's a diagram that shows the probabilities of multiple consecutive losses with a trading strategy that has a 40% chance of losing on any single trade.

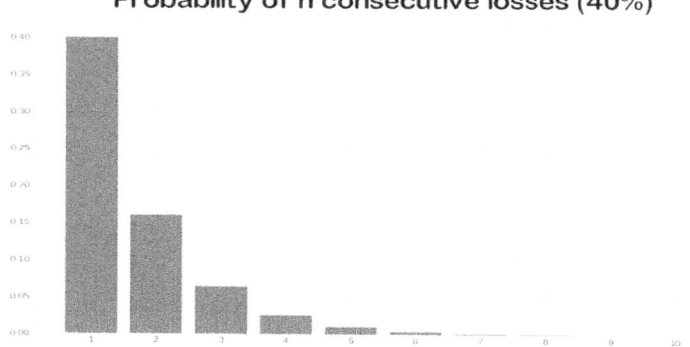

Probability of n consecutive losses (40%)

As you can see with a 40 chance of losing it is extremely unlikely that you will have more than a handful of losses in a row. So what can we learn from this? Firstly no matter how good your strategy is, losses do happen. You can't win all your trades. Therefore you have to implement solid risk management practices and keep the size of your losses under control.

The odds of having many losses or wins in a row is quite low. So if you often have more than 10 major consecutive losses, you should seriously start doubting the quality of your trading strategy. But always remember, even though the probability of winning 10 trades in a row is very low, the probability of winning on any single trade is not lower just because you won on the last 10 trades.

The confirmation bias is the tendency to seek out information that confirms your pre-existing beliefs. This is a bias that without a doubt, the vast majority of traders have been guilty of. After opening a trade it is only natural to continually seek out information that confirms your trading idea. You might look at dozens of indicators or social media posts and only focus on those that confirm your beliefs. Finding something that agrees with you is a good feeling and certainly can boost your confidence in a position. The problem is that by doing this you often ignore signs that your trade wasn't the best idea and something might be wrong. Instead, you convince yourself more and more that everything is fine. By searching Twitter for a ticker symbol you're almost guaranteed to find at least a few people that have the same market assumption as you. But this doesn't mean anything. One way to avoid confirmation bias in trading is by having a clear set of indicators and rules to follow for your trades. If you have such a clear set of rules and indicators, there is no need for you to go out and look for any other confirming signs. Furthermore, it is best to avoid social media as a trade decision making guide.

You might have heard about the law of large numbers that states that the average of a growing sample size converges to the actual mean of the total population. This is a very powerful rule in probability theory that allows you to estimate a population's parameters with large enough samples. But like the name implies, this only works for big sample sizes. This is where the fallacy of the law of small numbers comes into play. Most people intuitively use the law of large numbers incorrectly, namely with two small sample sizes. Let me give you an example. Have you ever tried a trading strategy for a handful of trades and then concluded that it doesn't work? If so, you have been guilty of using the law of small numbers. A few traits is not a big enough sample size to give you any significant information about the quality of a trading strategy. How you can avoid the law of small numbers? Well, you have to efficiently test the effectiveness of a trading system. The goal is to use this trading system for at least 20 trades. It might seem scary to use a new trading system for over 20 trades when you have no idea how good or bad it might perform. Therefore you should trim down your risk to a level so that you can easily afford to lose on all these 20 trades. Your goal with these trades is not to make money, but to test out the given trading strategy. When making these 20 trades try to be as mechanical as possible.

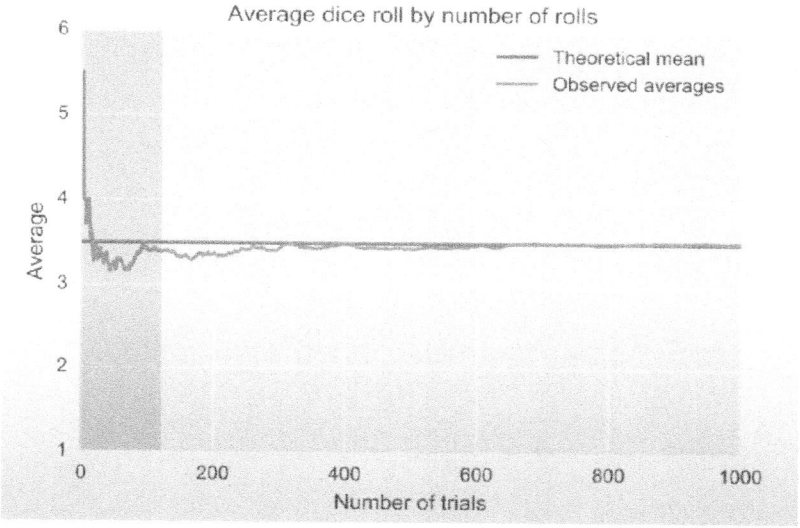

Create clear rules for every market scenario imaginable and follow these rules on every trade. If you don't have a clear set of rules to follow, you can't reliably test your strategy since there is no strategy to test. Furthermore make sure to keep a detailed and thorough trade journal. After every trade, track entry prices, exit prices, profit potential, money at risk, time in a trade and more. After you've followed all these steps for at least 20 trades, you're ready to evaluate the strategy. Ideally you should now have a rich collection of data on this strategy to evaluate it and make an informed decision on how effective this trading system is. I know that this might seem like a lot of work just to test the trading system but without having a big enough sample size, you can't really evaluate anything. Making a decision based on one or two occurrences, is like saying roulette has a 100% win rate because you won one round.

The next cognitive bias that we're going to look at is the survivorship bias. Wikipedia defines survivorship bias as "The logical error of concentrating on the people or things that made it past some selection process and overlooking those that did not, typically because of their lack of visibility."

Let's once again look at a couple of examples to better understand what this means. If you look around it is easy to arrive at the conclusion that most ETF-s Mutual funds and even individual stocks go up over time. But in reality, this is a wrong conclusion. That's because the universe of funds and stocks that you look at, is already skewed in one direction. One reason why stock did not go up but instead fell is that it went bankrupt. And a bad performing fund usually gets closed after a few years. In other words only those funds survive that performed well enough. So when you say that most stocks or funds go up over time, you aren't considering all those that didn't survive. Therefore the results obtained by only looking at survivors can be vastly flawed. To give you some data a Vanguard group study recently found that an investor in a large cap growth or value fund in 1997 stood just a 22% chance of finding a fund that would survive and outperform its benchmark through 2011. The problem of only considering a universe of investments that survived a certain selection process is especially common when back-testing and analyzing trading strategies on historical data. But also when analyzing success stories outside of trading, survivorship bias can be a big problem. The results of looking at shared trades of highly successful people, doesn't actually yield very significant results. Typically, many unsuccessful people also share these traits but they weren't considered in such a study which can dramatically skew the results. Often successful people succeed in spite of certain traits, not because of them. The phrase that history is written by winners very much also applies in business and financial markets. In general, when looking at and analysing investments make sure to think about that what you can't see. Is there a seemingly invisible filter that you are missing? If so, your results can be vastly skewed in an unwanted direction.

Correlation does not imply causation but sadly it is often treated as if it does. There are different types of this fallacies so let me cover three of the most prominent causation fallacies. The first is reverse causation. An easy example of this is the correlation between rainy days and the usage of umbrellas. When it rains people tend to use umbrellas much more. Does that mean that using umbrellas causes it to rain? Of course not. It's the other way around. This might seem like an obvious mistake, but often things aren't as clear. If for instance asset A and asset B are heavily correlated, does that mean that an opt move in A's price causes a reaction in B's price or the other way around? Another causation bias is neglecting the fact that the third variable might be the cause of two correlated variables. For example two oil stocks might be highly correlated but this doesn't mean that a move in one of the stocks causes a move in the other stock. Instead, a third variable namely the price of oil might be the cause for the moves in both of these stocks. Last but not least, two variables can also be correlated without having any causal link. In fact, if you have a big enough set of data, you're almost guaranteed to find some variables that are correlated purely by chance. One example of such a coincidental correlation is the correlation between per capita consumption of chicken and US crude oil imports. These two variables have a historic correlation of almost 90% over about 10 years. Nevertheless, I wouldn't use chicken consumption data to try to predict US crude oil imports. There are countless similar examples of seemingly nonsensical correlations. So going forward never assume that correlation means causality. Proving correlation is very straightforward, but proving causality is a totally different story.

Hindsight bias is the tendency of overstating the odds of an event that has already happened. Here is a great quote from Nobel prize winning Daniel Kahneman about hindsight bias. "A stupid decision that works out well becomes a brilliant decision in hindsight." Hindsight bias is especially common amongst traders. Way too many traders evaluate the quality of their trades based on their outcome. This is a very flawed way of evaluating your trades. A trade that has a 70% chance of making 200 dollars and a 30% chance of losing 100 dollars is without a doubt a great trade. No matter its outcome, even this trade won't work out three out of ten times. But that doesn't make it a bad trade. Sadly this is how many traders evaluate their trades. Hindsight bias is also the reason why technical analysis seems so attractive. Finding chart patterns on historical charts is very easy, but without the benefit of hindsight things aren't nearly as easy. If you ever felt that the past price move seemed so obvious, you have fallen prey to the hindsight bias buyers. To avoid hindsight bias, you need some way of evaluating your trades not based on their outcome. Instead you should focus on the quality of your decisions along the way. Did you have a clear trade plan and strategy? If so did you follow it? If not, why not and what could you do better next time? In general, it is best to have a consistent way of evaluating your trades that is not affected by the outcome of your trades.

Recency bias is the illogical way of putting more weight and importance to recent events, compared to historical ones. This can easily be observed by looking at the cyclical nature of markets. The longer a bull market is, the more and more people forget that prices don't only go up. Thus investors pay less and less attention to their risk, even though it should be the other way around, since the further prices rise the more they can fall. The same is the case directly after market crashes. This is when people typically over manage their risk because they overestimate the odds of future drops. This can be a great time to sell overpriced insurance products such as options and volatility.

A different bias that can be observed in the trading news business is the attribution bias. The attribution bias is the bias of constantly trying to assign some reason to an event, even if your reason has nothing to do with reality. Financial news companies are in the business of satisfying this bias. They seem to have an explanation for every single price move, even if their explanations sometimes are contradictory. Sometimes you can't break down a price move into a simple cause and effect relationship. But this doesn't stop us from trying.

The problem is that humans are very good at finding an explanation for almost anything, even if the explanation doesn't make sense. Basic traits on these explanations can do more harm than good. So make sure to be careful when looking at the reasons that financial news organizations assign to certain price moves. The best explanation for an up move, will always be that they are simply more buyers than sellers.

If you ever held onto a position far longer than you should, you have been guilty of this fallacy. The sunk cost fallacy is the tendency to refuse to stop an action because you've already sacrificed a good amount of money and or time into it. Sometimes it's best to just cut your loss than to further waste money and time on a project or trade. Some costs should not be a reason for you to stay in a trade. If you wouldn't open your trade at its current price level, you should not stay in it. Regardless of how much you already have lost. One way of combating the sunk cost fallacy is by having a clear trade plan with clearly defined exit points before you enter a trade. We have now covered a wide variety of different cognitive biases that can dramatically impact your trading and decision making in general. Let me now cover briefly look at how you can avoid these biases. First and foremost, it is already a good step in the right direction to be aware of that these biases exist. But sadly, simply being aware isn't enough to completely avoid them. In fact it is almost impossible to fully eliminate these biases from your life, since they are so deep ingrained in your human psychology. That said you can definitely do things that can reduce the frequency of them and thereby improve the quality of your decisions. One thing that can dramatically increase the likelihood of using these cognitive biases, is trying to make a decision under time pressure. So avoiding time pressure is another step in the right direction. One way of avoiding time pressure in trading, is by preparing beforehand. Instead of trying to improvise and rely on your intuition always have a clear trade plan before you open a trade. The trade plan should have all the information you need to mechanically carry out your entire trade. Besides a trade plan, a good trade journal is another way for you to improve upon your decision making and trading. Otherwise try to actively monitor yourself for these cognitive biases. Especially in situations where the likelihood of a bias is high, step back and rethink the entire situation from another perspective. Furthermore, avoid making important decisions when you're in a bad mood or not fully focused due to a lack of sleep. For instance if you are interested in learning more about this topic I highly recommend checking out Daniel Kahneman's book called "Thinking fast and slow".

In this chapter I will explain how you can develop a winning attitude in trading. But first of all, why psychology and trading even important. Well, trading is a very unique activity. It's unlike every other activity that you can imagine. In some cases even contradict some beliefs that we have acquired throughout our lives. Let me give an example of this. Most people think that the more work you put into something the better results you will get. For instance most jobs are paid on a per hour basis but this isn't necessarily the case for trading. Just because you spend countless hours analyzing the fundamentals, the technicals or anything else of an asset doesn't mean that you will make money. You may very well even lose money and a trade that you spend countless hours preparing. Trading is a very emotionally demanding activity. Seeing your hard-earned money vanish in front of your eyes isn't easy. But also huge gains do affect your emotions. Trading confronts us with constant uncertainty. May very well lose money on a day but you may also very well make money. It's not uncommon to see people lose weeks or even months of gains on one bad trade. Nevertheless, it is important to try to avoid emotional trading. Letting emotions influence your trading decisions can dramatically decrease your trading performance. It can be very hard to control your emotions when hard-earned money is on the line. There are five fundamental truths that can help traders to develop a winning mindset. First of all, anything can happen. In essence, the markets aren't anything else than millions of different people expressing their thoughts about different assets. People that think in assets prices low will likely buy, those that think in assets prices high will sell and others will wait for a better opportunity. But every single trader of these millions of people can impact the price. Therefore theoretically anything is possible. But even though everything is possible not everything is likely. The probability that an assets price will rise by hundreds of percent is relatively slim. However the probability is not zero. It is possible. This brings us to the second fundamental truth. You don't need to know what is going to happen next in order to make money. You don't only don't need to know what is going to happen next. You can't know what is going to happen next. We just learned that the markets aren't anything else then millions of people expressing their beliefs. If you know what's going to happen next, you would have to be familiar with the beliefs of all of these millions of people interacting with the markets. It's safe to say that this is impossible but that doesn't matter you can still make money in the markets. If you have the trading system with the true edge it really does not matter what's going to happen next? Well, the outcome of next trade is irrelevant. For example a casino has a true edge. The odds are on their side. Let's take roulette as an example. The casino has a higher probability of making than losing money on a game of roulette. However they do not know what's going to happen on the next roulette spin, nor do they care. They may very well lose money on the next spin of roulette. But that doesn't matter to them because they know that they will win in the long run. The same goes for your trading. As long as you have a trading system with the real edge all you have to do is stick to that trading system. The outcome of your next one two or even more trades does not matter. As long as you stick to your plan, the numbers will work themselves out in the long run. The next fundamental truth is that there's a random distribution between wins and losses for any given set of variables that define an edge. This goes hand-in-hand with the previous truth. Just because the odds are in your favour does not mean that you will be right. Let's look at our casino example once again. The odds of winning a game of roulette are strongly in the favor of the casino. However that does not mean that they will win guaranteed. They will still lose money on some games. If you really believe in a random distribution between wins and losses, could you really ever feel betrayed by the market? If you flip the coin and guess right, you wouldn't necessarily expect to be right on the next flip simply because you were right on the last. Nor would you expect to be wrong on the next flip if you were wrong on the last flip. Let's move on to the next fundamental truth. An edge is nothing more than an indication of a higher probability of one thing happening over another. Hopefully this is relatively simple by now. Once again I'd used the casino example to explain this. In a game of roulette, the casino has a higher probability of making than losing money. So that is their edge. The final fundamental truth is that every moment in the market is unique. If this wouldn't be the case, it would mean that every single person and entity that interacted with the market during a previous moment would have to do the exact same thing again. They would all have to enter and exit their positions just like last time. This is more or less impossible and therefore every moment in the market is unique. If a moment isn't unique you would have to know every variable which once again isn't possible. So what are the takeaways of these five fundamental truths? Well, first of all you do need a concrete trading system with concrete rules. Otherwise, you wouldn't have an edge and then trading would be pointless. Remember, random trading will lead to random results. Besides a trading system, you also need a trading plan. You should always create a trading plan before every trade. It's very important that you create your trading plan before you open a trade because that's the only moment where you still are able to think 100% rationally. After you enter a trade your hard earned money is at risk and then your emotions will influence your decision making. Some key components of your trading plan should be your max risk, your max reward, your risk to reward ratio, your exit point, your entry point, your adjustment point, your position size and ideally even more. If you truly believe in the five fundamental truths, you will automatically create a trading plan before every trade. For instance if you actually believed that you don't know what's going to happen next and anything is possible, you would always define your risk and cut your loss. If you believed in your edge and all the truth why would you do it from your trading plan. Why would you revenge trade or double up to make back the losses from a previous trade. Why would you ever feel emotional pain if you believed in your edge. Does a casino feel emotional pain just because it lost on a single game of roulette? No, and neither should you. The more specific your trading plan is the better. If you have trouble sticking to your trading plan write it down. In theory, your trading plan should be so concrete that you would be able to give it to someone else who then could execute the entire plan without having to ask you. The more specific a trading plan is, the less you will have to think about what you're going to do and thus you will trade more mechanically. Another tip for trading more mechanically is using trade alerts. If you know that they're going to exit or adjust a position if a price reaches a certain point, you can set an alert at that point. As soon as that price will be reached, you will get notified and can adjust your position without having to think about it. Alternatively, you could use automated orders like stop losses or take profit orders. But probably one of the most important takeaways is that you should trade small. You should never risk more than a few percent of your total capital on one trade. If you truly accept the risk before entering a trade and keep your position sizing small, you will never ever have trouble sleeping at night. Remember that you don't and can't know it's going to happen next and therefore it's not unlikely that your next trade will be a loser. If you risk all of your capsule at once and the next trade will be a loser, you will lose all of your capital at once. That's a disaster that you should never risk. This is also why casinos said betting limits. They know that they can very well lose on a single game of roulette. If someone wants to bet millions of dollars on a single game of roulette, the casino will likely decline. Because it knows that the odds aren't heavily in its favour. Their edge only really works in the long run when the number of occurrences is high enough. You should think the same way with your trading. So never risk too much of your capital at once. If you're currently familiar with the seemingly profitable trading system but somehow can't manage to be consistently profitable with it, it might be due to your mindset. So instead of trying to learn tons of new trading strategies, you could try to focus more on your psychology.

One of the worst mistakes beginning traders make is to not pay enough attention to their trade entries. Neglecting the importance of a good entry and exit can make a huge difference to your bottom line. In this chapter you will learn all the do's and don'ts of opening and closing trades. Before we get into the nitty-gritty of actually setting up the best possible trade order, let me first talk about how to set your trades up for success. One of the biggest mistakes that you can make is to not have a clear trading plan. Without a plan you're basically trading blind. To help you always have a trading plan from now on I'm going to present you a step by step checklist that walks you through every aspect to consider before sending any trade order. If you go through all these steps you should never again be in a trade that you don't know what to do with. Let's now go through this trading plan template. First of all I recommend taking a look at upcoming events. Even though this doesn't directly affect your trade looking at future events before opening a trade can save you from unwelcome surprises. Are there any upcoming dividend payments earnings or other upcoming events that might clash with your trade plan? Around these events stocks often behave differently and they normally would. So either be aware of this or avoid trading through these events.

Next, define your risk. Never open the trade without knowing your max loss. Way too many traders don't do this even though this is a must for you to be able to manage the risk. Besides defining your risk you should also define your reward. Have a clear profit target that tells you when to take profits. Without a clear profit target it's easy to tell yourself to wait for just a little more. Doing this will lead to winning trades turning into losing ones. After defining your max risk and Max reward is very easy to calculate your risk to reward ratio. So make sure to do exactly that. Actually calculating and seeing your risk reward ratio will give you more insight into the payoff of your trade. A good rule of thumb is that your risk to reward ratio is better than 1 to 2, but note that you should also take the probability of profit into account. It's totally ok that your risk is greater than your reward as long as your probability of profit is high enough. Furthermore, you should also define the time frame of your trade. Is it a day trade, swing trade or long term investment. You don't need to know the exact time that you're going to be in the trade but you should have an estimate of the trades time frame. Inside of your trade plan you should also have a concrete entry plan. This plan should entail your entry price, position size and how you want to open your trade. Do you want to open the entire position at once or slowly average into it? Lost as important is your exit plan. This should describe how you're going to close your position. This could include possible trade adjustments, your trade exit price and exit trigger. The most obvious exit trigger would be a certain price level. But it certainly isn't limited to that. You could for instance also use a timeframe, probability of profit, certain indicator values or the P&L of your position as an exit trigger. Moreover, your exit plan should include how you're going to close the position. Last but not least, a trade plan could also include other notes such as the motivation behind the trade, your directional assumption, a trade description or something else. Hopefully this template gives you an idea about what a good trading plan could look like. It's very important to create such a trading plan before you open your trade. This allows you to stay rational and clear-headed. As soon as you open your trade, you lose the ability to evaluate the position objectively. Furthermore it's a great idea to actually write down your trading plan. Especially for beginning traders this is a good exercise. With time you will be able to do this in your head, but like everything this requires practice. So even though writing down your plan takes time it will force you to really think about your trade. This is also a great counter against impulsive trades or Gamble's. If you ever again find yourself in the situation that you have no clue what to do with your trade, just take a peek at your trading plan and you will see the answer to this question. After you close a trade you should always ask yourself; did you stick to your trading plan? If you didn't, why not and what could you do better next time? If you did, was it a good plan or how could you improve the plan next time? Asking and answering these questions will allow you to continually improve your trading plans and thereby your trades. A great place to answer these questions is in your trading journal. Having a good trading journal is another great way to evaluate your trades without falling prey to cognitive biases and subjectivity. If you currently do not have a trading journal I highly recommend starting one as soon as possible.

Even though setting up an order might seem like an easy task, there are still are many things that you can do wrong. For example the biggest mistakes that many traders make is using market orders. A market order gives you the next available price. This will get you filled very fast but more often than not the price will be bad. So what should you do instead? Well, instead of market orders, use limit orders. Limit orders allow you to set a fixed price at which you want to get filled out. Either you will get filled at this price or you won't get filled at all. As long as just don't set your price too aggressively and the security is liquid enough, you will get filled at your desired price anyway. But even if your order isn't filled it is often better to miss a trade and to accept a bad entry price, since a bad entry price would mean more risk and less profit potential. To choose a good limit price it is important to understand how the "Bid-Ask Sread" works. The bid price is the highest price a buyer is willing to buy the underlying security for and the ask price is the lowest price a seller is willing to sell it for. The bid-ask spread is the sprint between these two prices. To get filled as fast as possible, you need to move closer to the ask price when buying and closer to the bid price when selling. For most securities however these prices change all the time. Therefore you can often get filled at the mid-price. That's also why I recommend always setting your limit order price at the mid-price to begin with. If this doesn't get you filled, you can always readjust later on. Ordering at the mid-price can save you thousands of dollars over the long run. Last but not least I recommend setting your orders to expire at the end of the current trading session. But if you don't want this you can always choose a good to cancel order. This order type will stay active until it is either failed or you cancel it manually. This is especially useful to automatically take profits on a given trade. For instance, if you know your profit target you can just send out a good to the concert order as soon as you open your trade and let the order sit. The same can be done for the downside with a stop loss. An alternative to good to the cancel orders are good to date orders. The only difference between the two is that good to a date expire after a certain preset days whereas the good to cancel order has to be concert manually unless it's filled. Some brokers even offer bracket orders. These are also known as one cancels other orders. Such an order allows you to send out two orders one to take profits and want to cut losses and as soon as one is filled the other one is automatically cancelled. This is a great way to automate your trading plan. It's hard to make discretionary trading more mechanical than this. Last but at least here are some tips to get feel it faster First of all, make sure to trade liquid securities. If you aren't trading liquid securities fails will take much longer and even worse, it will leave a lot of money on that due to a wide bid-ask spread. If you're trading options you could analyze option chains for options with high open interests and volume. Getting filled on these options is much easier than other ones. The next tip would be to scale into your trades. Instead of opening your entire position in one order break it down into multiple smaller orders. This can decrease field times dramatically. Note that you should only try this if your broker's commission structure doesn't charge you too much for each order. Otherwise, placing orders at route numbers can often help you since route numbers typically attract much more stop losses and limit orders than other prices. If none of these things help, you could always move your price closer to the bids or ask price. But only do this if the new price is still good enough. In summary, you should always have a clear trading plan and make sure you create this before your trade. If you don't know how to create a trading plan just use my template from the previous chapter. Furthermore, make sure to keep a trading journal so that you can track your progress and learn from your mistakes. Otherwise, don't use market orders but instead use limit orders. A good limit price to start with is the mid price. Last but not least focus on trading liquid securities with high-volume, otherwise you're just throwing money out of the window.

Conclusion

Thank you for purchasing this book. I hope this title has provided some insights on Bitcoin and cryptocurrency trading. Additionally, if you want to learn more about Bitcoin, Bitcoin mining, Blockchain and Cryptocurrency investing or trading, please check out the following books.

BITCOIN IS BLOCKCHAIN AND HERE IS WHY!
BITCOIN FOR BEGINNERS
MEET THE ARCHITECT OF BITCOIN AND BLOCKCHAIN: SATOSHI NAKAMOTO
CRYPTOCURRENCY INVESTING USING HOT & COLD WALLETS
CRYPTOCURRENCY INVESTING 17 PRIVACY BASED COINS YOU SHOULD KNOW ABOUT
BITCON AND CRYPTOCURRENCY TRADING FOR BEGINNERS

Lastly, if you enjoyed the book, please take some time to share your thoughts and post a review. It would be highly appreciated!

Made in the USA
Monee, IL
29 May 2021